When Sherry Harney talks about prayer, opened my eyes to fresh ways to commune benefit, too, from her biblical insights.

—LEE STR...... ...e Case for
Christ and *The Case for Faith*

Everybody prays. Everybody struggles with prayers. Sherry gives wise guidance for the prayer-filled life.

—JOHN ORTBERG, author of *All the Places to Go*

I have known Sherry Harney for almost thirty years. (We met in the church nursery!) If there is anybody who is qualified to lead us in the important subject of prayer and partnership with the Holy Spirit, it is my friend Sherry. Her spirit is so in tune with God and her pen so beautifully flows with words of inspiration. If you want to draw closer to God, put this book on the top of your list.

—RANDY FRAZEE, author of *What Happens after You Die*

This is my go-to book when talking to anyone about prayer. Sherry has done a marvelous job combining passionate personal experience, practical application, approachability, and biblical background. Some books excel in one, a few in two or three. I honestly don't know that I've ever come across a book that captures all four to the degree that Sherry Harney does in this excellent book.

—GARY THOMAS, author of *Sacred Marriage*

Sherry Harney is not just an author and speaker, she is a personal friend, the first person I think of whenever I need powerful prayer in my life. Sherry has steeped every aspect of her life in prayer and communion with Christ, and I have been blessed by her prayers for my family through the heights of joy and the darkest of life's valleys. If you want to learn to pray with fresh passion, biblical integrity, and eyes wide open to the world around you, let Sherry teach you.

—NABEEL QURESHI, author of *Seeking Allah,
Finding Jesus* and *No God but One*

This book is an invitation to experience the divine presence of God in a deeper, more intimate way. Read it to learn the unforced rhythms of doing life with God's Holy Spirit.

—SANTIAGO "JIMMY" MELLADO, president
and CEO of Compassion International

Simple insights are often the most revolutionary—this book has revolutionized my prayer life, through the simple invitation to pray "with eyes wide open," like Jesus did. Sherry smashes the shackles of popular misconceptions about prayer and sets us free into a breathtaking, biblical horizon, where we can pray at all times and in all places, attentive and attuned to the people and places around us, discovering our time with God is limitless.

—JOSHUA RYAN BUTLER, author of *The Skeletons
in God's Closet* and *The Pursuing God*

While there have been many books written on prayer down through the centuries, Sherry Harney has presented a fresh and encouraging way to pray. I have had the privilege of knowing Sherry for many years and she is one who truly lives out what she writes and teaches. She not only has a prayer life, she lives a life of prayer. This book accomplishes several things. First of all, it gives us a practical example of how to live out the Scripture, "to pray without ceasing." It also helps us to be alert to see what things and people God brings into our day. Most of all, however, this book is a beautiful invitation to keep company with Jesus, which is the true heart of prayer.

—MARILYN HONTZ, author of *Listening for God* and *Shame Lifter*

I love this book because it is much more than a manual on a fresh way to pray (though it is!). It is a recovery of the ancient biblical command to "be *alert* and always keep praying" (Eph. 6:18). Sherry Harney expertly and winsomely breaks down the artificial barrier between the sacred (eyes closed) and the secular (eyes open) and shows us how to live a seamless life in which living is praying and praying is living, and Christ is all in all.

—BEN PATTERSON, author of *God's Prayer Book*

I love this book! Sherry Harney helps the reader learn how to enjoy ongoing conversation with God—with eyes, ears, and lives wide open to him. As I read, I found myself wanting more—more of God and the intimate prayer life that he invites us into. Thank you, Sherry, for helping me learn to enjoy a richer prayer life.

—NANCY GRISHAM, PhD, author of *Thriving: Trusting God for Life to the Fullest*

This book is a rare gift. Most authors can inform. Good ones can inspire. In this book, Sherry Harney accomplishes a more challenging task: she invites. Each chapter is filled with a potent blend of profound reflection and practical wisdom. The combined effect for anyone who reads will be an enlarged spiritual appetite. Ultimately, Sherry helps us hear the Lord's invitation to draw near to him with our whole self and discover his presence and power in our everyday lives.

—ADAM T. BARR, coauthor of *Compassion without Compromise*

Organic
PRAYER

OTHER BOOKS IN THE ORGANIC OUTREACH SERIES

Organic Outreach for Ordinary People
Organic Outreach for Churches
Organic Outreach for Families
Organic Disciples

Organic
PRAYER

DISCOVER THE PRESENCE AND POWER OF GOD
IN THE EVERYDAY

Sherry Harney

with Kevin G. Harney

ZONDERVAN
REFLECTIVE

ZONDERVAN REFLECTIVE

Organic Prayer
Copyright © 2024 by Sherry Harney and Kevin Harney

Originally published in 2017 by Baker Book House as *Praying with Eyes Wide Open: A Life-Changing Way to Talk with God.*

Published in Grand Rapids, Michigan, by Zondervan. Zondervan is a registered trademark of The Zondervan Corporation, L.L.C., a wholly owned subsidiary of HarperCollins Christian Publishing, Inc.

Requests for information should be addressed to customercare@harpercollins.com.

Zondervan titles may be purchased in bulk for educational, business, fundraising, or sales promotional use. For information, please email SpecialMarkets@Zondervan.com.

ISBN 978-0-310-16152-3 (audio)

Library of Congress Cataloging-in-Publication Data

Names: Harney, Sherry, 1960- author. | Harney, Kevin, author.
Title: Organic prayer : discover the presence and power of God in the everyday / Sherry Harney with Kevin G. Harney.
Description: Grand Rapids, Michigan : Zondervan Reflective, [2024] | Series: Organic outreach | Originally published: Praying with Eyes Wide Open: A LifeChanging Way to Talk with God, Grand Rapids, Michigan : Baker Books, 2017.
Identifiers: LCCN 2023057817 (print) | LCCN 2023057818 (ebook) | ISBN 9780310161509 (softcover) | ISBN 9780310161516 (ebook)
Subjects: LCSH: Prayer—Christianity. | BISAC: RELIGION / Christian Living / Prayer | RELIGION / Christian Ministry / Evangelism
Classification: LCC BV210.3 .H3635 2024 (print) | LCC BV210.3 (ebook) | DDC 248.3/2—dc23/eng/20240131
LC record available at https://lccn.loc.gov/2023057817
LC ebook record available at https://lccn.loc.gov/2023057818

Cover design: LUCAS Art & Design
Cover image: © robertharding / Masterfile
Interior design: Sara Colley

Printed in the United States of America

24 25 26 27 28 LBC 5 4 3 2 1

In the pages of this book, you will meet many of my prayer mentors and heroes. Some are biblical characters, like Hannah and the apostle Paul. Others are great prayer warriors from the history of the church, like Brother Lawrence, Andrew Murray, and R. A. Torrey. Some of these people are friends and church members who have invested in my prayer life and modeled a passion for communicating with the Living God.

Among these great giants of prayer, two stand out in my life because they have spent time on their knees praying for me from the time I was in my mother's womb. Sherwin and Joan Vliem are my parents by birth and also my spiritual parents. Their authentic faith has shaped me, their trust in the Word of God has inspired me, their humility has formed me, and their prayers have covered me.

I can confidently say that my father and mother have prayed for me faithfully all the days of my life. My father has the gift of intercession. I have told my dad about needs of people he has never met and discovered decades later that he still prays for them daily. My mother has a pure faith in Jesus that trusts and believes without wavering. The two of them together have fortified me in prayer and taught me what a life guided by faith-filled prayer looks like.

I dedicate this book to Sherwin and Joan Vliem. So much of who I am, what I know, the way I love, and how I live for Jesus came from watching the two of them follow Jesus.

CONTENTS

Part Four: Praying with Lives Wide Open

INTRODUCTION

IT WAS A SNOWY and blustery winter day in Michigan, and I was out walking with my dad. Whenever I visit my parents, I do my best to enter into the routine and rhythm of their life, and my dad has a regular routine of walking four to five miles each morning, rain or shine, sleet or snow, right after his morning time in the Word of God and prayer. As we neared the end of our walk on this particular winter day, and knowing I would soon be heading back to my home in California, I asked him if we could pray as we walked. My father gladly agreed.

I immediately started praying but was surprised and a little shocked at what happened next. My dad bumped me, knocking me into the snowbank on the edge of the road. I instinctively knew what must be happening. I was sure my dad had knocked me out of the way to save me from a car sliding out of control on the icy roads.

But when I looked back, to my surprise and confusion, there were no cars on the road.

I hit the snowbank with a gentle thud, looked up at my dad, and asked, "What happened?" With a little chuckle he said, "I am so sorry, when you said, 'Let's pray,' I went into automatic prayer mode and closed my eyes." With his eyes closed, my dad had lost his balance and accidentally knocked me into the snowbank.

We both laughed as he helped me up. As we finished our walk, we had a rich conversation about the necessity, in many situations and circumstances, of keeping our eyes wide open and the dangers of closing them. The next morning, I received this email from him: "Dear Sherry, I thought about you this morning while I was walking. I prayed with my eyes open. I even prayed out loud. I learned from you that if I pray with my eyes open, my time with God is limitless."

Many of us have habits of prayer. We've been trained and taught to close our eyes, bow our head, and fold our hands. But there is nothing inherently biblical about this posture. And while these habits can be helpful to focus our attention at times, they can also limit our understanding and practice of prayer. The goal of this book is to help you discover the wonder, beauty, and joy of praying—not just at a specific time with a particular posture—but throughout the flow of daily life, as an organic and natural expression of your walk with Jesus. My passion is to see ordinary followers of Jesus grow into organic pray-ers who naturally talk to God, listen to God, and interact with him at all times, in all places, through all circumstances. For many of us, that begins by learning to pray with our eyes wide open.

Throughout this book I will use the phrase "praying with eyes wide open" in two distinct ways. Sometimes it will mean opening our eyes as we pray, just like I did with my father on that snowy day. When we do this, we become more aware of creation, people, beauty, and the needs around us. As we pray this way, our opportunities for prayer multiply.

Yet "praying with eyes wide open" can also be understood more broadly as we pray with greater awareness of God's presence, power, and work in the world. Our eyes might at times remain physically closed, but our growing awareness of God's will and desires opens us up to pray with greater passion and clarity.

Having our eyes open in both of these ways—physically and figuratively—will expand our prayer life, leading to a richer understanding and experience of the presence and power of God in the everyday moments of life. This is the kind of prayer God wants us to experience, organic prayer that flows naturally, like conversation between good friends. It may not happen right away, but my hope and prayer is that the stories and practices in this book will lead you to experience this type of prayer with the Lord as you grow in deeper friendship with him.

Part One

PRAYING WITH
EYES WIDE OPEN

PRAYING WITH EYES WIDE OPEN can become a lifestyle. This means shifting our thinking about prayer and at times keeping our eyes open when we talk with God. By making this small shift, we discover that we can pray at all times and in all places. When we do this, we will find ourselves praying more.

Praying with our eyes open also allows us to see what is happening around us and engage in prayer in new ways. Instead of closing our eyes to block out the world, we open our eyes, like Jesus did. We see the need and pain as well as the beauty and joy all around us. What we see shapes our prayers.

This is the life of organic prayer. Talking with God and listening for his voice becomes like breathing. We can be sitting in church, driving down the road, taking a walk, sitting in the middle of a business meeting, playing with our children, or doing anything, anywhere life takes us.

When we pray this way, our time with God is limitless and the power of God is unleashed in surprising new ways.

Chapter One

LIMITLESS PRAYER

If I pray with my eyes wide open, my time with God is limitless.
—Sherwin Vliem (my dad)

I WAS SPEAKING at a women's conference in the charming coastal city of Adelaide, Australia. Just as I was preparing to speak at the final session of this four-day event, a lovely woman came walking toward me. She seemed happy, but serious, and politely asked if we could spend a few minutes talking. I was heading out to catch a plane shortly after the session and knew there was a good chance I would not have time to talk when the session ended. My dilemma was that I normally don't engage with people's personal requests right before heading up to speak.

I lifted up a brief and silent prayer with eyes wide open: "Lord, would you have me spend a few minutes with her right now, because I don't know if I will actually have time after I speak?" I felt a gentle nudge in my heart and knew I needed to connect with her right then and there.

My immediate thought was that these few precious moments

were intended to serve her. To my surprise and delight, God's plan was to encourage me through this dear woman.

She told me she had no intention of coming to the conference, but a friend had invited her persistently and kindly, challenging her to make the time. After going to sleep one evening, she woke up in the middle of the night and could not get back to sleep. She felt uneasy about attending the conference, so she got on her computer and googled the name of the speaker: Sherry Harney. Finding a link to a message I had shared with the student body of Westmont College in Santa Barbara, California, she clicked the link and watched the entire chapel message.

Pausing at that moment in her story, she said, "Little did I know that what I would hear in that video would change my life!"

During the message, I had spent only a few minutes talking about the idea of praying with our eyes wide open, but God had taken this simple and profound idea and begun a transformation in her spiritual life and in the lives of her children. As she listened to the Westmont chapel message, the Holy Spirit mercifully pierced her heart. She began to understand, at a level deeper than ever before, that God is truly with her always. Her eyes were opened to the reality that she could talk with, commune with, and connect with God at any time—all the time. She came to see that praying with her eyes open was necessary if she were to increase her time communing with God.

With sober eyes, the woman looked at me and confessed she was serious about her Christian faith, but she had not been communicating with God throughout her day. With an even deeper sadness, she admitted she had failed to teach her children how to pray throughout their day. Prayer had become a thing to do a certain way at a certain time, but not a spontaneous and Holy Spirit–breathed part of each moment of life. With steely-eyed conviction, she looked at me and said, "This reality broke my heart, but I determined at that moment this will change, and I will attend the conference."

The morning after watching the chapel video, while driving her children to school, this precious mom taught her children the simple lesson she had learned the night before. She explained that they could pray anytime, with their eyes open. She declared the truth that God is with them at all times and in all places. And then she invited them to keep their eyes open, look around, and begin praying together as they traveled to school. As a family they talked to God, eyes wide open, hearts engaged with their loving Creator. It felt natural and good. In the following days she continued to invite her children into this sacred rhythm of natural conversation with God.

My new friend looked at me with tears flowing down her cheeks. "Now when we get in the car before heading off to school, my children ask, 'Mom, what are we going to pray about today?'"

She thanked me for helping her see what had eluded her for so many years. I asked her if I could have her nametag and let her know that I would put it on my desk while I was working on this book. I wanted her to know that the experience she had would be an inspiration to me as I wrote.

I believe that lives, homes, and communities can be transformed if God's people will learn to enter into limitless prayer. When we push the walls out, break from routine repetition, and pray without ceasing, God's presence and power are released.

WITH OUR HANDS FOLDED AND OUR EYES CLOSED

When someone says, "Let's pray," what do you do? Picture it in your mind right now. Many of us will close our eyes and fold our hands.

If we open our eyes and look around during a prayer, we might feel a little anxiety that someone will see us with our eyes open. If we lock eyes with another person who is also "peeking" during prayer, we might feel guilty and quickly close our eyes. For some reason, the consensus is that the proper posture for prayer is eyes closed and hands folded.

Yet there are many and varied postures for prayer modeled in the Bible. Shockingly, closing our eyes is not one of them. And just for the record, neither is folding our hands. So where did this idea begin?

While we can't know for sure, we do know that in the ancient world people often averted their eyes in the presence of a king or sovereign. This might be one reason people throughout history have closed their eyes while praying. It also seems likely that the pattern of eyes closed and hands folded in our modern culture began with parents teaching their children to pray. If our hands are folded, we can't poke our neighbor or grab food off a dinner plate. If our eyes are closed, we can focus better and avoid the many distractions around us. It's possible that, in many cases, these cultural factors could be the driving forces behind this common posture of prayer.

Yet while these might be helpful ideas for a child learning to pray, we should not feel bound to always fold our hands and close our eyes when we pray. Instead, we need to learn to pray in ways that help us deepen our walk with God, with our eyes wide open and our hands open to God and those around us.

To be honest, there are times when I love to pray with my eyes closed. Often, it's early in the morning when I am struggling to keep the distractions of the day's to-do list from overwhelming my racing mind. There are times when I focus better with my eyes closed. But many of us default to this single posture in prayer, so I want to offer a new paradigm, a new way to understand this amazing privilege we have throughout the day to pray continually. Praying with eyes closed is not wrong, but never praying with your eyes open may keep you from living out the scriptural exhortation to pray continually—and from its resulting blessings.

THE BIBLE AND OUR EYES

As I worked on this book, I read and reflected on passages throughout the Bible that speak directly or indirectly to the topic of prayer. I could not find a single passage where God *tells* someone to close their eyes to pray. Nor did I find a single place in the Bible where it states that someone closed their eyes when praying. I am not saying that people in the Bible or in the ancient world never closed their eyes when they prayed; I am simply making the point that the Bible does not command it or direct us to pray this way.

Instead, what we find in the biblical text are examples of people praying with their eyes wide open. A quick survey shows this is true in both the Old and New Testaments. When Abraham's servant went to Abraham's hometown seeking a wife for Isaac, we find him standing by a spring, praying for God to make his journey successful. As he prayed, he saw Rebekah come out with a water jar on her shoulder. The passage is clear. He *saw* the patriarch Isaac's future wife (Gen. 24:15) because he was praying with his eyes open.

When God's people were in the midst of battle, God gave them the victory. We read that God delivered them "because they cried out to him during the battle" (1 Chron. 5:20). Did they close their eyes as they were fighting to offer up this prayer? I think not. They did not fold their hands and close their eyes while engaged in fierce hand-to-hand combat. They prayed with their eyes open and their hands ready to fight.

When Jesus lifted up what has been called his High Priestly Prayer in John 17, we read that "after Jesus said this, he looked toward heaven and prayed" (v. 1). The Savior's eyes were wide open as he lifted up this prayer to the Father, his longest recorded prayer in all of the four gospels.

The Bible never gives a call or command to close our eyes when we pray, but there are many examples of people who prayed with their eyes open and God heard and answered those prayers.

THE BIBLE AND OUR HANDS

Similarly, the Bible never tells us to fold our hands when we pray. Instead, we read of people with their hands engaged, active, and lifted up in prayer. This does not mean we must always lift our hands, but it suggests that there are times this is wholly appropriate. There are many examples of this practice as well. Moses lifted his hands in prayer as he cried out on behalf of God's people (Ex. 9:29–33). Solomon spread out his hands toward heaven as he prayed (2 Chron. 6:12–13). David asked God that "the lifting up of [his] hands be like the evening sacrifice" (Ps. 141:2). The apostle Paul exhorted that people pray with holy hands lifted, without anger or disputing (1 Tim. 2:8). In addition, the apostles laid their hands on people as they prayed for them (Acts 6:6).

There is nothing wrong with folding our hands when we pray, but we can also lift our hands, lay them on others, and extend them to the God who loves us and rules the universe.

SIT, STAND, OR KNEEL

One principle I try to follow is that our outward posture should reflect what is happening in our inner person as we pray. The Bible does not prescribe a set body position for prayer but offers a variety of physical expressions that are appropriate. Since we are called to pray at all times, this makes sense. King David, in a time of humbly seeking God, "*sat* before the LORD, and he said: 'Who am I, Sovereign Lord, and what is my family, that you have brought me this far?'" (2 Sam. 7:18, emphasis added). Solomon, David's son, "*stood* before the altar of the LORD in front of the whole assembly of Israel, [and] spread out his hands toward heaven" (1 Kings 8:22, emphasis added). Just a short time later we read that "when Solomon had finished all these prayers and supplications to the LORD, he rose from before the altar of the LORD, where he had been *kneeling* with his hands spread out toward heaven" (1 Kings 8:54, emphasis added). Daniel, Paul, and Jesus all knelt in prayer (Dan. 6:10; Acts 20:36; Luke 22:41). When Jesus was in the garden of Gethsemane, in the shadow of the coming crucifixion, he was on his knees in prayer, a fitting posture in a time of agony and surrender.

A life of limitless prayer will mean learning to seek the face of God and engage in conversation with our Maker as we stand, sit, kneel, run, and lie down—in any and every position. What matters is not the one right posture but rather a right attitude that says we are always ready to pray.

LOOKING AND LONGING

One unique refrain that arose in the time of King Solomon was the call to the Israelites to turn their faces toward the temple in Jerusalem as they prayed. They were to pray toward the great city and this place where the very presence of God was said to dwell (1 Kings 8:30, 35, 38, 42, 44). They were called to look to the city and the temple as their hearts and eyes strained to see God, open and looking for God.

At the same time, Solomon prayed that God's eyes would be riveted on the temple and the people who were praying. He cried out, "May your eyes be open toward this temple night and day, this place of which you said, 'My Name shall be there,' so that you will hear the prayer your servant prays toward this place. Hear the supplication of your servant and of your people Israel when they pray toward this place. Hear from heaven, your dwelling place, and when you hear, forgive" (1 Kings 8:29–30).

Finally, in a massive crescendo of spiritual engagement, God appeared and spoke. He made a promise that expressed where his eyes would be: "When Solomon had finished building the temple of the Lord and the royal palace, and had achieved all he had desired to do, the Lord appeared to him a second time, as he had appeared to him at Gibeon. The Lord said to him: 'I have heard the prayer and plea you have made before me; I have consecrated this temple, which you have built, by putting my Name there forever. My eyes and my heart will always be there'" (1 Kings 9:1–3).

As the people looked toward Jerusalem, the temple, and ultimately toward God, God promised to look upon them. Not only are our eyes wide open as we pray, but we can be encouraged knowing God's eyes are wide open too.

WHEN EYES MEET

Picture your eyes meeting the eyes of God. God's eyes are on you. You sense he's always been protectively, lovingly watching you.

Does this elicit a powerful sense of relationship? In the book of Hebrews we read, "Nothing in all creation is hidden from God's sight. Everything is uncovered and laid bare before the eyes of him to whom we must give account" (4:13). God sees us at all times. He never looks away. That is one side of the relational equation. God's eyes are on us.

As we remember this, we are invited and encouraged to keep our eyes on God. In Psalm 123:2 we read, "As the eyes of slaves look to the hand of their master, as the eyes of a female slave look to the hand of her mistress, so our eyes look to the Lord our God, till he shows us his mercy." Our eyes should be locked on God, straining to see him in the normal flow of life. In the book of Hebrews we are challenged to "[fix] our eyes on Jesus, the pioneer and perfecter of faith" (Heb. 12:2). When our eyes are on God and we recognize that his eyes are on us, we can communicate with him and talk with him. We can pray.

PRAYING ON THE WATER

As I am learning to pray organically, in all places and at all times, I have people ask me to teach them what I mean by "praying with eyes wide open." This happened with a very sweet couple named Bob and Sherry, who invited my husband, Kevin, and me out boating one summer evening on Lake Michigan. It was peaceful and beautiful, and as we were navigating slowly along the lakeshore, we began talking about prayer and why praying with our eyes closed is almost reflexive for many Christians. They both admitted they had never prayed with their eyes open—at least not with other people around.

As I often do, I invited them right then to pray with me, but to keep their eyes open—especially since Bob was driving the boat! They started out feeling a little awkward. But as they looked around, they noticed the beauty of the lake and the magnificent setting around us, and their prayers turned to thanksgiving for God's artistic handiwork. Praise filled the air as we drank in God's glory all around us. Kevin prayed, thanking God for both Bob and Sherry, and as he prayed, he looked at each of them and made eye contact. They both made a point of not looking away. This was all new for them, and while it was strange, I knew we had entered a glorious prayer experience with them and the Lord.

After a heartfelt "Amen!" we talked about the experience. Both of them expressed delight, sharing that they felt as though they had opened a window after a long winter and were experiencing the fresh spring air. I encouraged them to continue praying this way as a couple and with their friends. We had experienced the sweetness of the Holy Spirit as we prayed together, making the boat ride and our time with them more special and memorable.

If you have never prayed out loud with other believers with your eyes open, I encourage you to give it a try. When you allow your eyes to meet another person's eyes as you pray for them, the Holy Spirit shows up and moves in a unique way. I have seen it happen over and over again. Praying with eyes wide open is not just about praying at all times. It also deepens our prayer and connects us with God and with other people on a level we may have never experienced before. Once we get past our habitual patterns and nervousness, it is natural, organic, and life-giving.

YOUR PRAYER JOURNEY

Over the coming week, try praying with your eyes open in yet another way. When you are in a group of people and someone says, "Let's pray" (it could be at a meal, at church, with friends, or in some other setting), don't close your eyes. Engage fully in your heart and join in with prayers out loud if appropriate, but keep your eyes open as you pray. Look at the person who is praying and seek to enter into the prayer in a fresh, new way. If someone happens to look at you during the prayer, don't feel guilty, just smile at them and keep praying.

I will offer a little warning as you get started. You might find yourself feeling awkward and even guilty if your eyes are open while praying at church or over a meal with family. Just press through it! Soon you will notice how your prayers take on new meaning when your eyes are open.

Chapter Two

PRAY CONTINUALLY

*I live in the spirit of prayer. I pray as I walk
and when I lie down and when I arise.
And the answers are always coming.*
—George Müller

AT FIVE YEARS OLD I encountered Jesus.

I had heard about him. I had prayed to him. But on a quiet Sunday, late in the afternoon, I lay on the sofa in our living room and personally met the Savior.

I know, I was just a little girl, but I assure you that he entered my life and has never left. Decades later his presence is sweeter and his power more profound. Since that day I have grown to love and hunger for his Word.

The Bible whispers and at times shouts the truth of heaven when I read it. Sometimes the words of Scripture lift my spirit and inspire me. They resonate with and penetrate my soul. At other times the teaching of the Bible confuses me and weighs heavy on my heart.

One such passage that troubled me for years and caused me to struggle is a seemingly simple two-word exhortation: "Pray continually" (1 Thess. 5:17). I wanted to obey God's call and follow his teaching, but how? How was I to pray without ceasing? How could I stay aware of God every moment and communicate my love with every breath? How could anyone measure up to this spiritual expectation?

As a young girl and later as a mom of three boys, I continued to feel the weight and pressure of this command. I could not do it. The very idea of praying at all times, in all situations, every moment of every day felt oppressive.

Then, after years of struggling with this passage, the Holy Spirit breathed a simple truth of understanding into my soul that changed everything. When the veil was lifted and I understood the real meaning of this passage, joy descended and prayers flowed with new freedom and passion. Here is what God taught me: It is not that we *have* to pray continually, it is that we *get* to pray continually!

This is not a simple matter of semantics. It is a spiritual reality, a paradigm shift of heavenly proportions. When we shift from requirement to privilege, from something we have to do to something we get to do, it changes everything, and I hope it is just as transformational for you. It is not that you and I have to pray every moment of every day. God will not be disappointed with you if you don't pray all the time. The amazing truth is that the Maker of heaven and earth invites us to commune with him at all times and in all places. When we are ready to communicate with the God of eternity, his eyes, ears, and arms are always wide open. His desire is that we would experience more of his presence and power in the everyday moments of our lives.

GOD IS NEAR

Prayer, in its simplest form, is about relationship. It is about being in the presence of the God who made us and loves us. When we learn to pray throughout the day, we remember we are not alone. We sense more deeply and intimately that God is with us in our pain, depression, sadness, and fear. He is also present at the heights of ecstasy, joy, and delight. From the valleys to the mountaintops, God is near, his door is open, he is present. With our eyes open, we see the world around us. We notice beauty, struggle, injustice, and kindness. We see God at work in the big and small things of life. And this moves us to prayer.

When we live with an awareness of God's glorious presence in each situation and every moment of our day, prayer becomes natural and organic, not processed and artificial. We talk with God as we would a friend, someone who is walking with us through the journey of life.

BIGGER THAN PRAYER

My journey of praying anytime and anywhere has done more than grow my prayer life. It has also transformed my understanding of God, deepened my intimacy with my Savior, grown my heart for the lost, and changed the flow and texture of each day. I see the needs of the broken in new ways. I feel my heart aligning with the passion of Jesus for those who have not accepted him as their Lord and Savior. With eyes wide open I have prayed with and for people who are spiritually wayward. It has not only drawn me closer to my Lord but also propelled me to look beyond myself and join him on his mission.

GOD'S GLORY AND OUR GOOD

Praying with our eyes wide open, literally and figuratively, brings glory to God, who receives eternal praise from heavenly beings as they cry out:

> "Holy, holy, holy
> is the Lord God Almighty,"
> who was, and is, and is to come.
>
> —Revelation 4:8

Acknowledging God in this way puts God in his proper place: first! When we seek to pray continually, we declare that he is Creator and we are creation, he is the Shepherd and we are sheep, he is the Potter and we are the clay. All prayer is first and foremost an acknowledgment of God's goodness and praise for who he is. It is for the glory of God.

At the same time, prayer is also for *our* good. When we pray with eyes wide open, we grow in our awareness that God is present, powerful, and protective. As our hearts and eyes tune in to the presence of the Living God, we discover that he delights in our desire for him. God rejoices when his children encounter him as their heavenly Father. Keeping God in the center of our attention glorifies him and benefits us.

The great eighteenth-century revivalist and preacher Jonathan Edwards described this connection of God's glory and our good expressed through prayer with these words: "With respect to God, prayer is but a sensible acknowledgement of our dependence on him to his glory. . . . Our prayer to God may excite in us a suitable sense and consideration of our dependence on God for the mercy we ask, and a suitable exercise of faith in God's sufficiency, that so we may be prepared to glorify his name when the mercy is received."[1]

In his book *God's Passion for His Glory: Living the Vision of Jonathan Edwards*, John Piper elaborates on this idea: "Prayer is calling on God for help; so it is plain that he is gloriously resourceful and we are humbly and happily in need of grace. The Giver gets the glory. We get help. That is the story of prayer."[2]

One of the great gifts of prayer is that it does two astounding things at the same time. First, and most important, it brings glory to God, who is worthy of all praise and honor. Second, and also important, prayer gives us what we need most: it connects us to the Lover of our souls. It fuses our hearts to the Father's heart, and we long for his glory to be seen by every person we encounter. These are all good things we need. Prayer is truly for God's glory and our good.

JESUS, OUR PERFECT EXAMPLE

Jesus is our example of all things good and beautiful. When we follow in the Savior's footsteps and watch his life story told in the Gospels, we discover that prayer saturated all he did. Jesus prayed continually as he journeyed here on earth.

Our Savior prayed in public. With a crowd of mourners gathered at the opened tomb of Lazarus, we read that Jesus lifted his face and voice toward heaven: "Then Jesus looked up and said, 'Father, I thank you that you have heard me. I knew that you always hear me, but I said this for the benefit of the people standing here, that they may believe that you sent me.' When he had said this, Jesus called in a loud voice, 'Lazarus, come out!'" (John 11:41–43).

Jesus also prayed in quiet and lonely places. "Very early in the morning, while it was still dark, Jesus got up, left the house and went off to a solitary place, where he prayed" (Mark 1:35). After the previous full and taxing day of ministry, teaching, and healing, Jesus felt the need to slip away to be with the Father.

Jesus prayed in the most public of settings and in quiet places as he retreated from the world and sought the face of the Father. When we pray throughout the day, we too may find ourselves communing with God when we are alone and when we are surrounded by people.

When Jesus was preparing to make a big decision, he cried out in prayer. Choosing his followers was a critical moment in the ministry of Jesus, so he made space to talk with his heavenly Father: "One of those days Jesus went out to a mountainside to pray and spent the night praying to God. When morning came, he called his disciples to him and chose twelve of them, whom he also designated apostles" (Luke 6:12–13). What a beautiful model! Like Jesus, we should talk with God about every important decision before we make it.

The Gospels also relate how the power of heaven moved through Jesus as he performed many miracles. A precursor to these life-changing moments was often prayer. "Taking the five loaves and the two fish and looking up to heaven, he gave thanks and broke the loaves. Then he gave them to the disciples, and the disciples gave them to the people" (Matt. 14:19). It's easy to miss, but notice that before the miracle of multiplying the loaves, Jesus gave thanks and acknowledged God's provision in prayer. More than five thousand men plus women and children ate this gift of bread, and there were even leftovers. Prayer marks moments when heaven intersects with earth.

Healing, too, was often accompanied by prayer. "He looked up to heaven and with a deep sigh said to him, '*Ephphatha!*' (which means 'Be opened!'). At this, the man's ears were opened, his tongue was loosened and he began to speak plainly" (Mark 7:34–35). Jesus, with eyes open, looked upward and spoke one word and the power of heaven was released.

Prayer was so important for Jesus that when a major spiritual experience was on the horizon, Jesus gathered people to pray with him. "About eight days after Jesus said this, he took Peter, John and James with him and went up onto a mountain to pray. As he was praying, the appearance of his face changed, and his clothes became as bright as a flash of lightning. Two men, Moses and Elijah, appeared in glorious splendor, talking with Jesus" (Luke 9:28–30).

Jesus knew he would soon face the trial and pain of the cross, so he asked these three friends to pray with him. God's answer was a revelation of his heavenly glory and a reminder of his true identity and mission in anticipation of his final days of suffering.

As we survey the life of Jesus, we should notice that prayer was not something Jesus reserved only for special and sacred moments. Yes, there were times when Jesus sought to be alone and experience the face of the Father in private intimacy, and so should we. But many of Jesus' prayers were also part of the natural flow of life, spoken in public settings and lifted to heaven with his eyes wide open.

JESUS' MISSION

Most corporations today have a mission statement, a declaration that expresses what they are all about and keeps them focused on their primary goal. In recent years, more churches are designing mission statements for the same reasons. But this is nothing new. Jesus had a mission statement that declared the focus of his life and the reason he came: "For the Son of Man came to seek and to save the lost" (Luke 19:10). Short. Sweet. Right to the point! Jesus was the Son of Man and he came to find lost sheep like you and me and bring us home. Once we have been found, we are now his followers and we adopt his mission for our own. We are called to pray with passion, love like Jesus, tell his story, extend his grace, and live like our Savior in every way we can.

Take a moment to reflect on your own life. What is your mission statement? Why has God saved you and what is the goal of your life? As you pray like Jesus and share his amazing grace and truth, know that God will use you to fulfill his plan for this world.

HOW PRAYER CHANGES AN ORDINARY DAY

It was a last-minute flight across the country for the funeral of a dear friend. In my search to find a ticket, I found a seat on Southwest Airlines, which meant I did not have a reserved seat. Southwest is different from most airlines in that they do not give you a seat but assign you a boarding group (A, B, or C) and a number. Your group and number determine the order in which you board, and when you walk onto the plane, you can take any available seat. Those who fly Southwest know the drill. If you are in group A, you are sure to get a good seat. Aisles and windows are plentiful! Group B boards next, and they tend to gobble up what is left of the window seats and a few remaining aisle seats. Those who fly Southwest joke that a C on your ticket stands for "center" because there is a good chance you will be snuggled into a center seat between the people in the A or B boarding groups.

On this flight, I had not only an A on my ticket for the first boarding group but also a very low number, which put me at the front of the line. While waiting, I found myself excited that I would be boarding early in the process. I was daydreaming about all the wonderful seating possibilities that would await me as I walked onto the plane. Should I take a window seat or an aisle? Maybe I could even find an exit row and really stretch out.

As the vast array of options ran through my head (only those in the A group have the luxury to ponder such choices), the Lord gently reminded me of a prayer I had lifted up earlier that morning. I had started my day talking to God in the privacy of my bedroom and had prayed that God would use me throughout the day, committing myself to serve him and others.

Suddenly, in the midst of my daydreams of A-group seating, the Holy Spirit whispered into my heart a convicting question: "Sherry, is this what your life has become?" Though the words were not audible, I knew what the Holy Spirit was saying. It had become all about me. I was consumed with thoughts of getting the best seat for *me*. I said a quick prayer, with my eyes wide open, as I was walking onto the plane. "God, please don't let my life be just about me. I want what you want." It was just a quick breath of a prayer, not complicated. I did not kneel down or close my eyes.

I can't say I heard a direction for exactly what seat I should take, but I knew God was up to something. So even though a wonderful and inviting exit seat was available, I chose to take a seat behind the exit row.

A short time later a man in his early thirties sat down in the row with me. We cordially greeted each other and went about our own business. Again, I silently prayed, "I don't know what you are doing, Lord. Maybe that stirring was just about me getting my heart right. I am here, and I am available." For the next hour we both focused on our own work.

All of a sudden we hit a dramatically turbulent patch of air. The plane dropped and rocked violently, and everyone on the plane got very quiet. I mentioned to the man next to me that I flew a lot and had never hit air quite that rough. We both nervously chuckled and then started chatting.

I asked what kind of business he was in. He had a very interesting job, and I continued asking lots of questions because I found his work intriguing. In the process of our conversation, he shared that his mother had died a few years back and it was a very disturbing time for him. Through this loss of his mom, he also lost faith. He went on to explain that during this time of struggle, he was seeking something more, something deeper and lasting. He told me he didn't have peace in his life and was investigating Buddhism as a possible answer to his heart's longing.

After listening to his story, I asked if he would mind if I shared how I find peace each day. He said he would like that, so I shared how having Jesus in my life has made all the difference to me. He listened intently, and at the end of our conversation, I realized we were about to land. I asked if he would mind if I prayed for him in his search for peace. He was very open.

I explained that when we prayed, we did not have to close our eyes. I told him I would pray quietly and would *not* be grabbing his hand. I lifted up a simple, heartfelt prayer, and when we were done, he reached out, squeezed my hand, and smiled.

I asked for his contact information and sent him some books. He responded with a very nice thank-you email, sharing that my prayers were appreciated and uplifting.

I had started my day in a time of private prayer. Later, while in line to get on my flight, that conversation with God continued, but this time it was more dynamic. I was in public, around other people, and God was challenging me to check my attitude and outlook. Following his lead, I ended up in a seat I would not have chosen, and that small shift opened the door—quite naturally—for a spiritual conversation. That led to another time of prayer—eyes wide open—with a man who was carrying pain and loss and seeking the peace that only God can give.

It struck me that this didn't need to happen just on airplanes while traveling. It could happen in many of life's ordinary situations. God is ready to use us and shine his light and love through the journey of praying at any and all times. Since that experience, I have tried to reflect each day on where Jesus has placed me so I can be a good, gracious, and gospel-sharing neighbor. Surprisingly, one of those places continues to be on airplanes. Each time I find 7A, 23C, or 57B, I know I will have an opportunity to be a good neighbor, whether that is during a short flight, a flight across the country, or a longer international flight. In each case, I pray for God to help me love my neighbor.

I've even added a fun twist to be more responsive to the Holy Spirit. When there is a need for someone to change seats or when the airline needs to move people around to shift weight and balance, I try to be willing to move, trusting that whoever I end up sitting next to might need a reminder or touch of God's grace. On one recent flight, when I agreed to be moved, I was placed next to a kind, thoughtful, curious atheist. I knew he was an atheist because in the natural flow of our initial conversation he asked me what I did for a living. When he found out I was a Christian author, he gave me a warm smile and said, "Oh, I am an absolute atheist."

This led to a civil, thoughtful, and lengthy conversation about the Christian faith. He had come to a point in his life while waiting in line for his chemo treatment for cancer when he decided God must not exist. One of the first questions he asked me was, "Do you really believe in a God who sends people to hell?" It was an honest question, asked with curiosity and kindness. I asked him if I could share a passage from the Bible and he was very open, so I read John 3:16–18: "For God so loved the world that he gave his one and only Son, that whoever believes in him shall not perish but have eternal life. For God did not send his Son into the world to condemn the world, but to save the world through him. Whoever believes in him is not condemned, but whoever does not believe stands condemned already because they have not believed in the name of God's one and only Son."

After we read this passage, we talked about how these words make it clear that our rejection of Jesus is the real issue at hand. God is loving and offers salvation to all, but we have a choice to make. Over the next two hours, I continued to lift up silent prayers as we talked theology and life. We spoke about leadership in the church, the needs of marginalized people in the world, and many other issues. I was able to share biblical truth with this thoughtful and kind man, and he was very open to hearing what I had to say.

Before our conversation concluded, I let him know I was delighted to meet him and really appreciated his honesty, curiosity, and kindness. Though he did not come to receive the love and grace of Jesus through that conversation, he commented that I had given him some things to think about. I am confident that God orchestrated this connection, and I believe that silent prayers before, during, and after this conversation have more power than we can comprehend.

As you begin each day, pray for encounters with people—with all sorts of neighbors in the various places you inhabit, work, and live. Keep your heart humble. Make sure there is room in your schedule to slow down. Then love generously and share freely. Organic prayers like these lead to organic conversations, and these in turn open the door for a powerful work of the Holy Spirit.

What is organic prayer? It begins with the understanding that we can share the beauty and truth that God loves us and wants to be with us—all the time. We invite lost people to encounter God through prayer and to experience his wonderful presence wherever they are at. Organic prayers offered up in the course of everyday life help spiritually disconnected people realize that God longs to have a personal and intimate relationship with them. In a world where people feel isolated and distant from others, this realization is powerful.

As my dad said, "When we pray with our eyes wide open, our time with God is limitless." Life becomes an adventure, and prayer guides us from moment to moment. Our "ordinary" days and moments become extraordinary experiences when they are saturated with the presence and power of God.

YOUR PRAYER JOURNEY

Over the coming week, take time every day to pray with your eyes open. Make a point of praying in situations where you would normally not be praying. Pray silently and try praying out loud (when the situation is appropriate). Take note of how you are praying more often and how prayer is moved and guided by the things God places right in front of your eyes.

Chapter Three

RELATIONSHIP MATTERS

*In simple prayer we bring ourselves before God just
as we are, warts and all. Like children before a loving
father, we open our hearts and make our requests.*
—Richard Foster

THE DAY STARTED like any other, but by the time I went to
bed that night, I would look back and realize I had received one
of the greatest gifts of my life. It was 6:00 a.m. on September 7
and it was my thirty-fourth birthday. I was enjoying some quiet
time with God on the sofa in my living room before my three
boys would wake up and bring their joy, energy, and volume to
our home. I heard a stirring and looked up from my Bible to see
my middle son quietly trying to sneak past me. Josh, our then
five-year-old, was headed to our bedroom. I was curious why he
was up this early and wondered if he had remembered it was my
birthday.

I listened intently, trying to figure out what he was up to. I could hear that he had gone into my bedroom closet, and I remembered there was a box filled with cards for all occasions tucked in the corner, but I did not know if Josh was aware of this. Josh appeared several minutes later—a card in one hand and a little unwrapped blue box in the other. But it wasn't just any box. It was his *favorite* school box.

He walked over to the sofa where I was reading and quietly handed me the card and box as he said, "Happy birthday, Mom." I was touched by the kindness of my little boy so early in life and so early in the morning. Even if there had been nothing in the box, the thoughtfulness of his actions had already brought great joy to my heart.

I looked at his little face. "Oh, Josh, thank you so much."

I opened the card (which I still have) and smiled. Instead of addressing it to MOM, he had written the card to WOW. Josh was still working on getting his *W*'s and *M*'s figured out, and it was quite early in the morning. He signed the card, "I Love You." There were all sorts of cards in that box in the closet, and I was impressed that he had found a birthday card rather than a sympathy card.

As I thanked Josh for the card, he just smiled. I held the little gift box on my lap, covered with pictures of racing cars and classic cars. Josh sat quietly as I opened it and looked at the contents. There were four gifts in his special school box. As I looked at them, I realized each item reflected Josh's love for me.

I took each gift out of the box and held it in my hand, overwhelmed by a deep sense that this was a special moment of love between a son and his mother. The first item I held was his favorite little Matchbox car. I turned to Josh, thanking him for such a sacrificial gift. I told him that I knew this was his favorite car, and he nodded.

The second gift was a quarter. This was all the money he possessed at the time. "Josh, how special that you would give me all the money you have."

The third gift was a handheld toy that he always took with him whenever we traveled in our car. It was a little pinball game. This was in a time before video games, cell phones, or electronic gadgets were used to entertain kids while traveling, and he loved this little travel toy.

I thought to myself, *Wow, could this gift get any better? His favorite school box, all the money he had to give, his favorite Matchbox car, and his special travel toy.* You can imagine the heart of a mother receiving such a loving and sacrificial gift.

As I looked back in the box to retrieve my final item, its significance was not as obvious as the others'. I picked up the item and held it in the air so both Josh and I could see it.

It was a set of children's plastic play handcuffs.

I knew there had to be some significance to this gift, but I couldn't think what it might be. I had worked as a second-grade schoolteacher for a few years, so I used my teacher skills to unravel the mystery. Kindly, I asked him, "Josh, what were you thinking when you put this in my special gift box?" He spoke quietly, "Well, I was thinking since today is your birthday, maybe you could put one handcuff on one of your wrists, and I could put the other one on my wrist, and we could spend the whole day together."

Tears welled up in my eyes. "Oh, Josh, thank you so much. I would love to spend the day with you." And we did!

That birthday experience has since become a lasting picture of love that I continue to remember and share with others. In that moment, the Holy Spirit impressed a single thought on me: *You know the joy you feel right now toward your son? That's how I feel when you want to be with me, to talk with me, to encounter me.*

I knew God was teaching me through Josh's gift box and was over-joyed that my son would give with such sacrifice. I was also touched that what he wanted more than anything that day was just to con-nect with me.

With each passing year of my life, I learn more about prayer. But that experience with my son Josh seared a truth deep in my soul. Prayer is not first and foremost about making lists, getting our words exactly right, reciting memorized supplications, or using a particular posture. It is about developing a deep and vital relation-ship with the God who made and loves us. It is about coming to our heavenly Father and saying, "I want to be with you, all day long!" When this is our heart condition, our words and even our silence become prayer, for we are connected (handcuffed, if you will) to the God who loves to be with his children.

OUR THEOLOGY INFLUENCES OUR PRAYER

Prayer is more about the God we pray to than the exact words we pray. When we understand this truth, when it sinks in, our prayer life is transformed. Everything about prayer hinges on what we believe about who God is. Our theology will move us to prayer, or it will drive us away from him. We need a proper view of God, and the pictures we carry in our hearts can make all the difference. If we see God as an angry, aloof, absentee landlord who launched our small planet into space and left us to our own devices, we will not pray. Or we will pray only out of obligation or a sense of duty. Why bother? If we pray to such a stern and distant deity, our prayers will be guarded and cautious at best, and fearful at worst.

On the other hand, if we see God as he is—loving, staggering in his patience, and shocking in his forgiveness—we will run to his arms. When we see God with clear vision and eyes wide open, prayer is not a chore but a natural desire. When we see God as he is, we want to be with him, we love to talk with him, we ask if we can be handcuffed to him all day long, every day. When this happens, prayer is a never-ending conversation with the one who loves us beyond description and whom we love more with each passing day.

I grew up in a churchgoing family. I loved the fellowship, the truth proclaimed, and the songs we sang. They were often hymns, and one of my favorite songs was "In the Garden." As I thought about walking and talking with Jesus in the garden, I could feel his closeness. Each time I lifted up this hymn, I not only felt close to my Savior but also wanted others to meet Jesus too. As I grew spiritually, my heart ached for those who did not walk with him, talk with him, and know they were precious to him. As we grow in prayer, we feel the closeness of our Lord and we long for others to meet Jesus and follow him on this same wonderful and intimate journey.

GOD IS CREATOR

Our prayers become passionate and powerful when we understand that God is not only the Creator of the universe but also our Creator. He is personal. In Genesis we see God shaping and forming the first people and breathing life into their lungs (2:7). God's creating process was intimate. In the book of Psalms, David declares, "For you created my inmost being; you knit me together in my mother's womb. I praise you because I am fearfully and wonderfully made; your works are wonderful, I know that full well" (Ps. 139:13–14).

When we grasp that the Creator of the heavens and earth was also intimately involved in making us, we can believe that he knows what is best for us. We will also want to be near him and commune with him.

In the book of Isaiah, we hear the heart of God cry out to his people. They have wandered from his arms, forgotten how to pray, and forsaken their Maker. Instead of seeking God, they have embraced idols and acted unfaithfully. With a passionate longing to bring his people back to his loving arms, God reveals the empty vanity of idols and declares exactly who he is:

> Listen to me, you descendants of Jacob,
>> all the remnant of the people of Israel,
> you whom I have upheld since your birth,
>> and have carried since you were born.
> Even to your old age and gray hairs
>> I am he, I am he who will sustain you.
> I have made you and I will carry you;
>> I will sustain you and I will rescue you.
>
> —Isaiah 46:3-4

In these two brief verses, the Creator teaches his children at least three distinct things that should inspire us to pray. First, *he carries us*. Idols have no life, they must be carried, and they are a burden to those who believe in them and must tote them around. If you read further in Isaiah 46, you will find a clear description of both the uselessness of idols and the burden they cause: "They lift it to their shoulders and carry it" (v. 7). In stark contrast, our God carries us in our times of pain, loneliness, and brokenness. As in the well-worn poem "Footprints in the Sand," when we look back at the hard times of life and discover that only one set of footprints can be seen, we might despair and think that in those moments God has left us. But the poem goes on to remind us that at those times, God wasn't absent, he was carrying us. This is the picture God paints in Isaiah. There are times, from our childhood and into old age, when the God who created us picks us up and carries us through the storm. We have all had moments of loss, sorrow, sickness, and pain. In those times we rightly say things like, "If God had not carried me, I would have never made it."

In this same passage in Isaiah, God assures us that *he sustains us*. These are the times we keep walking on our own two feet, but the presence and power of our Creator helps us endure the challenges and weather the storms. In these moments we don't need to be carried, but we need to be infused with his divine power and aware of his intimate presence. This empowers us to walk on and keep following him.

In addition to carrying and sustaining, God also *rescues us*. Because he made us and loves us, there are times when God delivers us from ourselves or the actions and harm others might bring upon us. I am convinced that on the other side of this life we will see the countless ways God has intervened on our behalf, often without our knowledge or awareness. Of course, the greatest rescue we can experience is when Jesus died on the cross and bore our sins, shame, and the judgment we deserved. There is no greater rescue than being delivered from our sin and its consequences.

If we live each day with a biblical and personal conviction that our Creator carries us, sustains us, and rescues us, we will be naturally compelled to communicate with him. Prayers of praise will flow from our hearts and lips. Cries for help will be frequent because we will know how much he loves to deliver us. We will regularly offer up confession of our need and brokenness. When our eyes are open to see the love and care of our Creator, prayer flows naturally and freely.

GOD IS FATHER

When Jesus taught his followers to pray, he encouraged them to address God with these words: "Our Father in heaven, hallowed be your name" (Matt. 6:9). Jesus himself called God *Abba*, an intimate word that means "daddy" or "father" (Mark 14:36). The apostle Paul tells us that we, too, can address God using this same name, *Abba* (Rom. 8:15). In 1 John we are taught, "See what great love the Father has lavished on us, that we should be called children of God! And that is what we are!" (3:1). God is our Father, and through faith in Jesus we become his sons and daughters. What an amazing truth! When we see ourselves as loved children, we will be compelled to talk often with our heavenly Father.

Jesus paints a vivid picture for us of God's fatherly love and provision: "Which of you, if your son asks for bread, will give him a stone? Or if he asks for a fish, will give him a snake? If you, then, though you are evil, know how to give good gifts to your children, how much more will your Father in heaven give good gifts to those who ask him!" (Matt. 7:9–11). This comparison is intentional and compelling. Jesus wants us to realize that even though human parents are broken by sin, they still provide for their children and extend care and love to them. How much more, then, will a perfect heavenly Father provide for and bless his children? When we see God as the perfect Father whom our hearts have always longed for, we will pray with new confidence, trusting in his goodness and provision for our needs.

Through the years I have heard people say that the image of God as a father is not helpful for those who have been abandoned, abused, or hurt by their earthly fathers. Some feel that speaking of God as Father can even be hurtful and we need to abandon that understanding. On the contrary, I believe we need to reclaim what the world has broken. If we have a marred view of our earthly fathers because of abuse or pain, we need to grasp a true understanding of God as a good and perfect Father even more. My heart goes out to those who have not had fathers who loved or provided for them. If that has been your experience, it is my prayer, even now as I write, that God by his Spirit will restore in your heart a right picture of your heavenly Father. Please know you have a perfect Father in heaven who sees you as his beloved child.

Some years ago my husband, Kevin, led a team that conducted Sunday worship services in a local jail. On one of these visits, the chaplain pulled Kevin aside and explained to him that any "father" language when referring to God would not be helpful and should be avoided. It happened to be Father's Day, and Kevin was feeling led by the Holy Spirit to do a whole sermon about God as our perfect and loving Father.

My husband faced a dilemma. Would he listen to the jail chaplain or the Holy Spirit? You can probably guess what happened. Kevin boldly taught the men in the jail, all three cell blocks, that they have a loving, faithful, ever-present, forgiving, and powerful Father in heaven. He shared the truth that none of us have perfect fathers, and some of us have absent or very poor earthly fathers. But the good news is that we all have a Father in heaven who is perfect and we can always trust in him. That Sunday the men responded with joy, tears, and excitement. When they realized they had a Father who knew everything about them and still loved them, they wanted to pray and talk to this Father. At all three services the men came forward to be prayed for in greater numbers than at any time before.

When we have a relationship with God, we can draw near to him with joy-filled confidence and speak to him in prayer. As his children, we cry out, "*Abba*, Daddy!" We tell him our joys, fears, victories, and defeats and know he cares about them all, because our heavenly Father loves his kids.

THE TENDER MOTHERLY
HEART OF GOD

The Bible never uses the term "Mother" for God, and we are not called to address God as Mother. But the Bible does use several beautiful and powerful images to help us understand God's gentle care, and some of these images reflect the tender heart of a mother. The prophet Isaiah records the heart and words of God when he writes, "As a mother comforts her child, so will I comfort you" (66:13). Earlier in Isaiah, the prophet writes, "Can a mother forget the baby at her breast and have no compassion on the child she has borne? Though she may forget, I will not forget you!" (49:15).

When Jesus laments over Jerusalem, he cries out, "Jerusalem, Jerusalem, you who kill the prophets and stone those sent to you, how often I have longed to gather your children together, as a hen gathers her chicks under her wings, and you were not willing" (Matt. 23:37). Just as a hen gathers her chicks and protects them, so God watches over us. In the book of Hosea, with sobering words the prophet paints a picture of God disciplining the people of Israel like a bear robbed of her cubs (Hos. 13:8). As we deepen our prayer life, pictures of God's tender and loving motherly heart will also draw us close to God in prayer.

GOD IS SHEPHERD

In the ancient world of both the Old and New Testaments, the work of a shepherd was familiar to all. Shepherds led, protected, and provided. Good shepherds loved their flocks and would die for the sheep they cared for, and God often presented himself as the Shepherd of his people. Isaiah writes, "He tends his flock like a shepherd: He gathers the lambs in his arms and carries them close to his heart; he gently leads those that have young" (40:11). What a picture of tender care and gentle love! This is the God we talk to every time we pray. In Psalms we are invited to worship, kneel, and engage with God as the sheep of his pasture:

> Come, let us bow down in worship,
>> let us kneel before the LORD our Maker;
> for he is our God
>> and we are the people of his pasture,
>> the flock under his care.
>
> —Psalm 95:6-7

In one of the most beloved and familiar passages in the Bible, the Twenty-third Psalm, we see a powerful picture of how we can relate to God as our Shepherd. David, a man who knew a lot about shepherding, wrote these words, inspired by the Holy Spirit. Though they might be familiar to some of you already, take time to read them slowly and remember that this is describing the God you speak to when you pray:

> The LORD is my shepherd, I lack nothing.
>> He makes me lie down in green pastures,
> he leads me beside quiet waters,
>> he refreshes my soul.
> He guides me along the right paths
>> for his name's sake.
> Even though I walk
>> through the darkest valley,

I will fear no evil,
>   for you are with me;
your rod and your staff,
>   they comfort me.

You prepare a table before me
>   in the presence of my enemies.
You anoint my head with oil;
>   my cup overflows.
Surely your goodness and love will follow me
>   all the days of my life,
and I will dwell in the house of the LORD
>   forever.

—Psalm 23

Kevin and I live a couple of miles away from the Fort Ord National Monument, which includes more than fourteen thousand acres of hills and eighty-six miles of hiking trails. It is all protected, public land. When we are not traveling, we have a Saturday morning tradition of doing a six-mile hike in the hills, and it has become a sacred time for us. We connect and catch up as we talk with each other. We spend time praying for our family and friends, our church, our community, and the world. We pray naturally, with our eyes open, and find it refreshing on many levels. It is always a highlight of our week.

One other reason this weekly ritual has become special for us is that we often experience a reminder of God as our Good Shepherd. Grazing on those hills there happens to be a flock of sheep. They are there to keep the wild grasses down, but they have provided us with frequent reminders of spiritual truths.

Every time I spot the sheep, I also look for the shepherd. It is a vast area of land, but I know the shepherd will never be far away. His eyes are always on his flock. Whenever I scour the hills looking for him, I find great delight and feel a sense of relief when I see him.

One day we noticed the shepherd was walking a few hundred yards ahead of us with one of his dogs. We had never seen him away from his sheep, so we looked around to see where the sheep were. We eventually found them some distance away, being well taken care of by the dogs.

The shepherd was clearly on a mission, and we wondered out loud, "Could he be looking for a lost sheep?" Moments later, off to our right, we saw him find the missing sheep. It appeared unhealthy, clearly lost, and a little sick. With tears filling my eyes, I watched as the shepherd directed the sickly sheep back in the right direction, calling him forward at times, and when needed, physically picking him up and pushing him where he needed to go. It was beautiful to see him caring for each of his sheep, unwilling to let even one of them go!

When we recognize that God is our Shepherd, we understand that he provides, guides, refreshes, protects, blesses, and prepares a place for us. And knowing this compels us to talk with our Good Shepherd. We learn to trust him at a deeper level and love him with greater passion. When we encounter God as our heavenly Father, we run to his arms and call out to him, *Abba*. When we are stunned by the reality that our Father is the Creator of the universe, we thank him for fashioning us and for being intimately involved in the smallest details of our lives. A theologically accurate view of God enables us to grow in our relationship with him, and this in turn moves us to pray.

YOUR PRAYER JOURNEY

Over the coming week, try a whole new way of praying. Take a morning or evening when you can find a few minutes alone, stand as you pray, turn your hands upward, and look toward heaven. Then pray, speaking out loud. In your prayer, address God as Creator and thank him for all he has made, including you. Next, address him as Father and praise him for adopting you as his child through the sacrifice of Jesus on the cross. Ask for power to live faithfully as his loving child, trusting his goodness and provision. Finally, address him as the Good Shepherd and pray for his leading in your life and for ears that hear and recognize his voice and guidance. Let this become an organic and natural part of your prayer life, as you learn to pray with your eyes wide open to the truth about God.

Chapter Four

POWER IN PRAYER

*Prayer is the key that unlocks all the storehouses
of God's infinite grace and power. All that God is,
and all that God has, is at the disposal of prayer.*

—R. A. Torrey

YEARS AGO I heard a Christian comedian, Ken Davis, talk about how Christians are like sheep. Ken had designed a T-shirt with a picture of Jesus and a sheep, and it had a lamb walking on its hind legs right in front of a ferocious lion and a menacing wolf. Both predators are glaring at the little lamb. Their eyes say one thing: "Lunch!" But walking next to the lamb is Jesus, holding the lamb's little hoof as they saunter past the intimidating carnivores.

In a text box over the lamb's head, the fluffy and vulnerable lamb has a few words to say to the lion and the wolf. And though it's a humorous picture, these words capture a deeper theological and biblical truth—that presence and power are linked together. The lamb simply says, "I'm with him," and points to Jesus. The lamb understands something we often forget, that we are safe because of the one who is with us. Presence and power are interconnected in the life of Christians, and this means that God's power becomes our power when we draw near to him. When we pray, we live in God's presence with greater awareness and will see God's power unleashed as we walk with the omnipotent Son of God.

PRESENCE AND POWER ARE INTIMATELY CONNECTED

In the previous chapter we reflected on the presence and person of God as our Creator, Father, and Shepherd. Each of these aspects of God's identity speaks of his intimacy with us. What we must also learn is that the power we need is always God's, never ours. Powerful prayer is not about leveraging, controlling, or convincing God of what he should do. It is not about speaking memorized scripts or clever incantations. It is about living in the presence of the one who has all the power.

Power is released when we focus on who we are praying to more than what we are praying about. The closer we live in fellowship with God and dwell in his presence, the more his power flows in our lives. God's sovereignty is absolute, his will is immutable, and he is worthy of our absolute devotion. The key to unleashing God's power through prayer is learning to live in God's presence. The two are inseparable, and God's presence is the key that unlocks God's power.

I AM WITH YOU

Moses learned this truth when God called out to him from within a burning bush on Mount Horeb. God spoke to Moses, telling him to return to Egypt and confront one of the most powerful leaders on the planet at the time, Pharaoh. Not only was Moses called to stand face-to-face with this mighty king, but he was also instructed to tell Pharaoh that God's people were leaving Egypt. Keep in mind that they were Pharaoh's slave labor for his massive construction projects. Moses's eyes were wide open to the challenge he faced. He knew this would not go well from a human perspective. But his eyes were open to the greater reality of God's presence with him, and he knew that with God anything was possible.

In an amazing encounter at the burning bush, Moses and God talked. It was a prayer encounter! Moses asked, "Who am I that I should go to Pharaoh and bring the Israelites out of Egypt?" (Ex. 3:11). God's answer seems strange. Instead of explaining who Moses was and how he was the right man for the job, God simply declared, "I will be with you" (v. 12). God's answer was to assure Moses of his presence, thereby guaranteeing him the power Moses needed. The focus was not Moses but God. "Moses, all you really need to know is that I will be with you!"

As a follower of Jesus, when I go through a challenging time and find myself anxious and worried or feel the fear descending and darkness clouding the sky, I hear God say something similar to my heart, "I will be with you." When Kevin and I hit a bump on the marital road we travel together, and I know God's call is to die to myself, I hear God's voice again, "I will be with you." When a family member or friend is struggling to make sense of a trial they are experiencing, I wonder how I can help. Again, God speaks, "Sherry, I will be with you and give you what you need to help that person." Like Moses, I remember God is with me and I can press forward. It is not about my strength, my insights, or my wisdom. It is about the God who is with me.

My prayer is that you will hear the voice of God. He is with you. He really is. Just ask him! Focus on who *he* is, not who *you* are. We all have limits; he does not. You might lack the power to make it through—in fact, you probably do. But when you pray with your eyes open to his presence, you inevitably hear him reassuring you that he is present. With God at your side, you are never alone. "If God is for us, who can be against us?" (Rom. 8:31). His power, through his abiding presence, is always enough.

I AM

Moses was not done having a Q&A session with God. He next asked God what he should say to the leaders of the people of Israel if they pushed back and did not believe that God had spoken to him: "Suppose I go to the Israelites and say to them, 'The God of your fathers has sent me to you,' and they ask me, 'What is his name?' Then what shall I tell them?" (Ex. 3:13). In the ancient world, a name meant everything. Moses knew the leaders would want an explanation of exactly who was calling them to rebel against Pharaoh. Who is this God who claims he can overpower the mighty king of Egypt, and why should they trust Moses to lead them?

God's answer to this question was similar to his answer to the first question. He says, "I AM WHO I AM" (Ex. 3:14). God declares, "I am the God who is." Here, God is speaking of his being, his nature. God goes on to tell Moses that he is "the LORD, the God of your fathers—the God of Abraham, the God of Isaac and the God of Jacob" (Ex. 3:15). God explains that he is the one who is with us at all times. He had been with the patriarchs and had led them for centuries. His presence and power would continue to be with his people because he is the eternal I AM.

When Moses felt inadequate and weak, he asked God, "Who am I?" and God's response was, "I am with you." When Moses asked, "What is your name?"—in essence, asking "Who are you?"—God responded by saying, "I am." In both cases, God assured Moses of his presence, and this held the promise of power to make it through whatever he would face. God answered both questions the same way: "I am with you."

PRAYER UNLEASHES HEAVENLY POWER

As you and I walk through each day with our eyes open to the presence of God, we will also see his power unleashed. But first, we must pray. Again, presence precedes power. Could it be that we do not experience the power of God because we have not prayed? Dallas Willard once said: "Learning to pray in the power of God is the primary place we learn to live with the power that God gives."[3] Seeking to live in the power of God without praying in power opens the door for us to grow proud or to have an inflated sense of our own abilities. We begin giving ourselves credit for God's great works. Our human hubris is staggering, and when we taste God's power, it can be intoxicating. We must be ever aware that the power unleashed in and through us is from God and is not our own.

When we forget this truth, we start thinking and acting in subtle or overt ways like we are the source of the work that God has accomplished. When we pray in power and trust in God and not our own abilities to deliver, answers come, and when they do, we can be certain that only God could have accomplished the powerful deeds we see.

If we want to see heavenly power in our lives, homes, churches, and the world, we must learn to pray for his power to work in and through us. We are delighted when God answers our prayers and he gets the praise. When we pray in this humble trust, living in the power of God becomes normal, not an anomaly. As we give God the glory for what he does, he unleashes even more.

AS IT HAS ALWAYS BEEN

All through the history of the Bible, heavenly power is unleashed when the people of God open their eyes, see a need, and ask God in prayer, unwilling to give up or let go until he answers. The great Wesleyan Methodist preacher Samuel Chadwick wrote, "There is no power like that of prevailing prayer—of Abraham pleading for Sodom, Jacob wrestling in the stillness of the night, Moses standing in the breach, Hannah intoxicated with sorrow, David heartbroken with remorse and grief, Jesus in sweat of blood. Add to this list from the records of the church your personal observation and experience, and always there is the cost of passion unto blood. Such prayer prevails. It turns ordinary mortals into men of power. It brings power. It brings fire. It brings rain. It brings life. It brings God."[4]

Prayer brings God! I love that. And God always brings his power, because he is unbounded power.

A cursory survey of the Bible shows this to be true from beginning to end. In the opening books of the Bible, we see that almost every significant character prays in power and sees answers to these prayers. The great patriarch Abraham cried out on behalf of King Abimelek and God responded with healing power (Gen. 20). Isaac prayed for God to open the womb of his wife, Rebekah, and she conceived twins (Gen. 25). Jacob prayed and wrestled with God and received a heavenly blessing (Gen. 32). Joseph prayed to God as a slave in a foreign land and God raised him up to the highest place in all the land, next to the king (Gen. 39–45). Judgment was falling on the people of Israel for their rebellion, and Moses prayed to God and the disaster ceased (Ex. 32). Joshua prayed and the sun stood still (Josh. 10). Gideon prayed and God prepared the way for victory (Judg. 6). Naomi prayed for God's blessing on Boaz and he received Ruth as his wife; they are both found in the genealogy of Jesus, the Savior of the world (Ruth 2 and 4; Matt. 1:5).

This continues throughout the Old Testament, as Hannah prayed and received a son, Samuel (1 Sam. 1–2). Then Samuel, the great prophet and judge of Israel, in his farewell speech prayed for the nation to be spared judgment for their hard hearts, and God answered his prayer (1 Sam. 12). Kings like David and Solomon prayed and saw heavenly glory released. Prophets like Elijah, Elisha, Jeremiah, and Isaiah prayed and God moved. Leaders like Nehemiah, Ezra, and Daniel cried out to God and saw heaven intersect with earth, and divine power was unleashed as walls were rebuilt, worship was restored, and deliverance was experienced.

The story of the New Testament continues this witness to the power of prayer. The church prayed for Peter while he was wrongly imprisoned, and God sent an angel to release him (Acts 12). The apostle Paul prayed for the early churches, and those churches helped plant other congregations that have passed down the legacy of the gospel to the bodies of believers we gather with today. Jesus prayed and the dead came to life (John 11). We not only see story after story of the power of prayer in the Bible but also find direct teaching on this topic. In his letter to the Ephesian Christians, the apostle Paul writes this prayer: "I pray that the eyes of your heart may be enlightened in order that you may know the hope to which he has called you, the riches of his glorious inheritance in his holy people, and his incomparably great power for us who believe. That power is the same as the mighty strength he exerted when he raised Christ from the dead and seated him at his right hand in the heavenly realms" (Eph. 1:18–20).

The power the Father makes available to us in prayer as we walk with his Son is nothing less than the power that raised Jesus from the dead. This resurrection power is available to you and me. This is why Dallas Willard warns us that *living* in God's power must begin by *praying* in power.

God is ready to do things in and through you that will bring him glory and amaze you. The power God wants to release in our lives is too much for us to handle. But if we know it is his power, if it comes through bold and humble prayer, God will get the glory. In the chapters ahead, you will discover many ways to pray in power. As you learn to do this, you will likely see amazing results. Be quick to give God all the praise, honor, and glory!

YOUR PRAYER JOURNEY

Over the coming week, pray before you walk into situations you know will be challenging, tough, or potentially conflict oriented. Ask God to let you know his presence and his power in the midst of these times. As you live through these situations, pray with your eyes open. Of course, pray silently, but intentionally and consistently. In particular, address God as the great I Am who is with you at all times. Ask him to help you see his presence and sense his leading in these challenging times of your life.

Part Two

PRAYING WITH
EARS WIDE OPEN

LORD, *hear my prayer,*
listen to my cry for mercy;
in your faithfulness and righteousness come to my relief. . . .
I spread out my hands to you;
I thirst for you like a parched land.

Answer me quickly, LORD;
my spirit fails.
Do not hide your face from me
or I will be like those who go down to the pit.
Let the morning bring me word of your unfailing love,
for I have put my trust in you.
Show me the way I should go,
for to you I entrust my life.

—Psalm 143:1, 6–8

OFTEN, PEOPLE ASK: Is God speaking? But that's the wrong question. The real question we need to ask is this: Are we listening? Do we hear the voice of the Creator of the universe? Are we attentive to the whispers of the Holy Spirit? Do we let God's Holy Word shape and transform our lives?

When we listen attentively, we will learn to recognize the voice of our Good Shepherd. Knowing his voice allows us to enter holy conversations and engage with God in new ways.

Chapter Five

GOD IS SPEAKING

Then you will call, and the Lord will answer;
you will cry for help, and he will say: Here am I.

—Isaiah 58:9

IN THE OPENING VERSES of the first chapter of the Bible, we read, "And God said . . ." (Gen. 1:3). With these words, the Lord of eternity began to speak all things into existence. In the last chapter of the Bible, God is still speaking. He says, "It is done. I am the Alpha and the Omega, the Beginning and the End. To the thirsty I will give water without cost from the spring of the water of life" (Rev. 21:6). At the consummation of all things, God is again speaking. From beginning to end, the Scriptures reveal a God who speaks, engages, and communicates with his creation and guides the people he made and loves.

Through decades of walking with Jesus, I have learned that God is speaking. Sometimes he whispers. At other times he shouts. At all times God is present and he desires to talk with you and me.

IN THE BEGINNING

God speaks in very personal ways. He does not give vague and obscure direction but crystal-clear leading for his people. The first man, Adam, learned this when his Maker spoke: "The LORD God took the man and put him in the Garden of Eden to work it and take care of it. And the LORD God commanded the man, 'You are free to eat from any tree in the garden; but you must not eat from the tree of the knowledge of good and evil, for when you eat from it you will certainly die.' The LORD God said, 'It is not good for the man to be alone. I will make a helper suitable for him'" (Gen. 2:15–18).

When I read these words, I am struck by at least four things God spoke to Adam. Each one reveals something about God and about us as his people.

*I am the God who **provides**.* Trees, trees, beautiful trees. Laden with fruit and pleasing to the eye and the taste buds. God tells Adam—and all of his children through the ages—that he provides what we need and even more because he loves us.

*I am your **protector**.* Beware of the poison that is in one particular tree. Don't eat it. It will kill you! God warns his first children and continues warning those in the lineage of the human family: sin destroys. God protects us with clear warnings.

*I have a **purpose** for your life.* Even before their fall into sin, God gives his children meaning and purpose by giving them a garden to work and keep. In the same way, God loves us and gives us meaningful labor and a reason to get out of bed each day.

*I delight in your **pleasure**.* Not only does God give his people sweet fruit, but he provides companionship and the pleasure of intimacy—a man and a woman together in a stunning garden. God commands them to be fruitful and multiply (Gen. 1:28; 2:25). God intends pleasure for his beloved people.

As it was in the beginning, it is now, and so it will ever be. God speaks to his creation with boldness, clarity, and grace. The question is not, "Does God speak?" The real issue is whether we are willing to listen. (We will get into that topic in the next chapter.)

Years ago when Kevin and I served in youth ministry, there was a young student who came from a difficult background. He placed his faith in Jesus, and we watched as his life ignited with passion for God and a desire to live for Jesus. We gave him a Bible and he devoured the Scriptures. For the first three or four weeks of his new life in Jesus, he read the Bible for more than an hour each day. The words of the Bible were making sense, and it was clear God was at work as he experienced transformation.

One day he stopped reading. He just shut the Bible and put it down. When we asked why he was no longer reading his Bible, he did not say, "Because it is hard to understand." Nor did he say to us, "I don't really get anything out of it." This was his answer: "As I read the Bible, it tells me to stop doing things I like to do. It also points out things I should start doing that I am not sure I want to do. It is making me very uncomfortable." What profound honesty! He did not struggle with hearing God speak. He struggled with how clearly the Holy Spirit communicated to his life through the Bible. On a happy note, after some prayer and a kind challenge, he was back to digging into the Word of God on a daily basis.

WHAT DO WE MEAN WHEN WE SAY "GOD SPEAKS"?

When some people hear statements like "The Lord told me" or "God said," red flags pop up and theological alarms go off in their minds. We understand that whenever we talk about God speaking, this language means different things to various groups of people. Some faithful followers of Jesus believe God speaks only through the clear teaching of the Bible. In their theological framework, God stopped communicating in other ways once the Bible was completed and we had this revelation in our hands. Their understanding of the Latin term *sola scriptura* is that the Bible is not only the supreme authority for all matters of doctrine and practice but also the only way God speaks today.

Other committed Christians believe God still speaks in a variety of ways. Jim Samra, a pastor, teacher, and theologian, wrote a book that presents God speaking to his children in many, various ways. The title of the book says it all: *God Told Me: Who to Marry, Where to Work, Which Car to Buy . . . and I'm Pretty Sure I'm Not Crazy.* Not only is that a mouthful, but it also reflects a specific theological position that says God still speaks today in many ways.

I believe the Bible is the final and absolute authority for all we believe and do. We measure everything by God's Word because it is absolutely true from beginning to end. If we ever have a sense that God is speaking to us, and what we hear is contrary to the teaching of the Bible, we are not hearing from God. The Holy Spirit will never speak, lead, or direct in a way that is contrary to the teaching of the Bible.

At the same time, I believe God speaks in a variety of ways that affirm and fit consistently with his Word. In the Old and New Testaments we see God speaking in many ways to his people, and I see no biblical evidence that God now limits himself to only one form of communication. What we must learn is to use the Bible as our measuring rod for all other times we believe God is speaking. As Christians we do not change our beliefs based on personal experience. Instead, we shape our lives to the clear teaching of the Bible.

GOD IS SPEAKING

I discovered this truth in a new way when I learned I would need a major surgery. At the time, I was training for a 25k run and my doctor said I would have to skip the race because he needed to perform surgery on me around the same time as the race. I love to run and had been training for six months, so I was very disappointed. The race was only a few weeks away, and I would have to miss it.

My youngest son, Nate, sensed my disappointment, so he made me an offer. He was only ten years old, but he challenged me to do the race on my own the weekend *before* my surgery. "Mom, you can do the race, and I will ride next to you on my bike." Somehow, one of the race organizers got wind of my "pre-race" race and my upcoming surgery and told the local paper my story. The next thing I knew, the *Grand Rapids Press* was interviewing my son and me and sharing my story to inspire other runners.

As I was preparing for my personal version of the "River Bank Run," I was also preparing for my surgery, so I prayed a lot as I ran. I am not a big fan of surgery, but who is? I had been through other surgeries and always seemed to have a difficult time coming out from under the anesthetic.

During the weeks prior to learning of my need for surgery, a particular psalm had often been on my mind. I believe the Holy Spirit kept putting Psalm 27, particularly the first verse of this psalm, on my heart as I found myself reading it and meditating on it as I ran. I love the whole psalm, but the first verse stuck with me: "The LORD is my light and my salvation—whom shall I fear? The LORD is the stronghold of my life—of whom shall I be afraid?" Through these powerful words of Scripture, God was breathing hope and confidence into my heart. I listened to the voice of God through his Holy Word and knew he was speaking to me.

As I continued training, now for my pre-race experience, my eyes were open to the glory of God's creation and the greatness of his majesty in the trees, the sky, and the landscape all around me as I ran. God revealed himself through the intricacies and expansiveness of his world. Again, I knew he was speaking and my confidence rose. It was springtime in Michigan, and as God was bringing the earth back to life after the harsh winter snows, it reminded me that he could certainly heal me and bring me back to full health after the surgery.

As I whispered my fears and frustrations to God about my upcoming surgery, I could hear the Holy Spirit whisper back, "I am with you. I have created you. I will never leave you or forsake you. You are my beloved daughter." Over and over, the simple truths I had learned from the time I was a little girl and all through my adult life came flooding back into my heart and soul. God was speaking again, reminding me of what I knew to be true.

In addition to all of this, God began to speak through my circumstances. People who had read the article in the newspaper shared words of encouragement with me. God used that article and my upcoming surgery to inspire others who were moved to pray for me, speak words of blessing, and cheer me on. God used my surgery and suffering as a witness to people that God is near and cares about each one of us.

The night before my surgery, my subsided fears seemed to rear their ugly head again. I remember praying to God, asking him to comfort me once again, and God spoke in a sweet and humorous way. My son Nate, who had encouraged me to run the race on my own, decided to motivate me yet again. He knew I was nervous about undergoing anesthesia and was anticipating a rough recovery time. He also knew I was worried that I would get up in the middle of the night and absentmindedly take a drink of water, which was forbidden before surgery. So, with tender care while I was sleeping, Nate tried to encourage me to finish a different kind of race.

I woke up in the middle of the night as I had expected, but as I got out of bed, I felt a piece of paper under my foot. Nate had placed it on the ground next to my bed, knowing I would find it there. As I read the note, I was staggered by God's goodness, speaking yet again to me through my son's encouragement. On the top of the sheet of paper Nate had written in large letters,

Psalm 27 Verse 1
The Lord is my light and salvation—whom shall I fear? The Lord is the stronghold of my life—of whom shall I be afraid?
Mom, Remember when you're out of surgery I will be praying for you. God will be with you. I love you, from Nate.

I had never mentioned Psalm 27 to any of my boys. Yet here was Nate, quoting Psalm 27 to me—the very same Scripture I had felt the Holy Spirit prompting me to read and reflect upon. I believe the Spirit of the Living God was speaking through my son. Right there, in his ten-year-old handwriting, were the very same words God was speaking to me through Scripture to reassure me of his presence and power.

As I entered the bathroom, overwhelmed with God's goodness to me, I found another note taped to the faucet: "Don't drink!" My son had thought of everything. And when I reached to lift the cover of the toilet seat, there was one more little note: "Don't even think about it!" I laughed. God was not only speaking to me through my son but also easing my worry through Nate's sense of humor.

MANY WAYS

I believe God speaks to us in many different ways to guide us, comfort us, challenge us, and draw us nearer to his heart. My journey of preparing for surgery revealed a number of ways God speaks.

God speaks through the **Bible***.* On my journey, God used a particular psalm to comfort, strengthen, and bring me confident hope as I prepared for surgery. This should not surprise any follower of Jesus. The primary way God speaks, in all generations, is through the Bible. The apostle Paul wrote these words, inspired by the Holy Spirit: "All Scripture is God-breathed and is useful for teaching, rebuking, correcting and training in righteousness, so that the servant of God may be thoroughly equipped for every good work" (2 Tim. 3:16–17). If you want to hear God speaking to you and giving directions for every aspect of life, make a practice of opening the Word of God each and every day of your life.

The wisest Being in all the cosmos has given us his Word. Reading the Bible every day will attune our spiritual ears to God's voice. If you ever have times when you feel far from God and don't know where to go or what to do, immerse yourself in the beauty and truth of the Bible. When you open this glorious book and read it, you are hearing from God. If you are not a big reader, I suggest you use a Bible app (BibleGateway or YouVersion are great options) and have your smartphone read the Bible to you. I know people who begin each day by listening to Scripture, and it is transformational for them. In the ancient world, almost no one owned a Bible and many people could not read. But they heard the Bible read to them. Bible listening is not a cop-out—it is retro!

Through the years I have found that nonbelievers are often open to prayer in their times of need and struggle. I have found that many of my friends who are not yet followers of Jesus appreciate me telling them about specific psalms that speak to their personal situations. I explain that the whole book of Psalms is a collection of ancient but contemporary prayers that can help us express our hearts to God.

Psalm 23 is familiar to many people who don't go to church or follow Jesus. It is one of the psalms I encourage people to lift up daily as they walk through their dark valley. It is amazing how often this practice of praying a psalm draws a person's heart to God and opens the door for deeper spiritual conversations. God speaks through the Bible, even to nonbelievers, and as they learn to pray the Scriptures, God can speak truth to their hearts.

God declares his glory through **creation**. As I trained for my race, ran, and prayed, the beauty and wonder of God's creation spoke to my soul and reminded me of his faithfulness. In Psalm 19 we read, "The heavens declare the glory of God; the skies proclaim the work of his hands" (v. 1). God's glory is revealed in oceans, mountains, deserts, butterflies, and even falling leaves.

When I was in college, I hit a time when I was desperate and depressed. My first semester had not been the experience I had hoped for or anticipated. It was a major disappointment and left me disillusioned. A friend of mine named Maria was a resident director (RD) at a neighboring college, so I sought her out for some counsel. I shared some of the events that had contributed to this time of struggle and my doubts of God's direction and care. Maria reminded me that God cares about me, and that in the midst of what appeared to be a chaotic time, God cared about both the big and the little details of my life. She pointed to Scripture and assured me that God knows the number of hairs on our heads, he knows when one sparrow falls, and he is the Creator of all. She then encouraged me to go outside and look at a leaf—one single leaf. She suggested I reflect on the detail and intricacy that God had placed in that one leaf. I did what she suggested. I went outside and picked up a leaf and looked at it carefully, and God spoke to me. Through the power of the Holy Spirit, God gently reminded me that if he spent time designing this one leaf in such a magnificent way, he had done the same with my life. My hope was restored; I knew God was speaking personally to me. I was reassured and my spirit was lifted.

*God guides and directs through his **Holy Spirit**.* One reason I made it through that time of struggle was because I sought God and asked him whom to seek for help. The Holy Spirit kept putting Maria's name on my heart. It made sense to me that God would direct me to her. I knew that as an RD of a Christian college she would be able to help me process my complicated emotions and thoughts. I don't believe the idea to seek her out came from me; it was the Spirit of God directing me to the right person, the person he wanted to use to help me through this difficult time.

God spoke to his prophet Elijah through the still, small voice of his Spirit (1 Kings 19:12–13). Jesus assured us that his sheep recognize the voice of their Good Shepherd (John 10:4). There are details of life that the Bible does not address specifically, but God wants to direct our steps in these areas. The Bible is clear that God delights when a man and woman are joined together in marriage, but it does not tell us exactly whom to marry. God cares about where we live, where we go to school, how we use our resources, and every other detail of our lives. We need to seek the Spirit's leading in life's big and little decisions.

Organic prayer is a dynamic process of communicating with God and inviting him to lead every step we take. Over the past decade, I have developed a practice of asking the Holy Spirit to lead me to people who need to experience the love of the Father. In the morning, as I begin my day, I will often lift up a simple and sincere prayer, "Lord of compassion, if you want to show your love to someone this day through me, I am available." In my heart, I am open to being used by the Lord in the lives of other Christians and also as I interact with people who do not know the Savior. It is amazing how many days God answers this prayer. When we are willing and available, the God of compassion will open our ears to hear his gentle whisper, "Share my love with this person."

God leads, and sometimes stops us, **through circumstances**. If you read the book of Acts, paying special attention to how circumstances directed both Peter and Paul, you will find that open and closed doors became an indicator of God's leading. Sometimes a person would invite them to minister—an open door. At other times a town would become violent and drive them away—a closed door. Over and over, the early church leaders let circumstances become one of the ways they would sense the Lord speaking and directing.

When Kevin and I moved from Michigan to central California, it wasn't easy. All of my family and many of my closest friends lived in Michigan, and by God's grace we were able to live and minister there for two decades and raise our boys near my family. But then God called us to move and serve a church on the West Coast. As I struggled with sadness and mixed emotions, I heard the Holy Spirit whisper in my heart to read Psalm 23, the great Shepherd Psalm. God further impressed upon my heart that I should read this every morning as I got up. I had a distinct sense that if I did not read this daily, I was not being obedient to God's whisper in my life at that moment. I didn't know how many mornings that meant; I just knew I was to start a regular practice of reading this psalm. So I read and prayed Psalm 23 daily for more than two months, and God used that psalm to comfort me and prepare me for a new chapter of life and ministry. He reminded me that he was a Good Shepherd, leading me to green pastures and heavenly peace.

When we arrived in California, we could not find a house we could afford or qualify to buy. After months of prayer and work, a door opened and we got just the right home for this next chapter of life. After we had settled into our home, I was chatting with a church member and was delightfully shocked when he said, "I don't know if you know this, but John Steinbeck, the famous American novelist, used this exact valley as the setting for one of his short stories." I asked him what it was called and he replied, "The Pastures of Heaven." It immediately struck me that in the valley where we now lived I was surrounded by lush green hills and pastures. At that moment, I had no doubt God was speaking, and I knew we were in the right home. We had arrived at our green pastures. I also understood why God had spoken months earlier in a still, small voice and had told me to read Psalm 23 every day. Now it all made sense. I also knew that his word was now complete for me and my daily practice of reading Psalm 23 could end.

*God confirms his will and ways through **people**.* During the preparation for my race and surgery, God spoke to me through my son. God also used Maria to encourage me during a difficult time away at college. Both Nate and Maria loved Jesus and were responsive to the promptings of the Holy Spirit. Throughout the Bible, God uses people to speak. One of the most shocking examples is when God spoke through King Cyrus, a pagan leader (Ezra 1:1–4; 5:13–16; Isa. 44:28–45:1). If God could direct and speak to his people through a nonbeliever, how much more can he speak through those who love and follow him?

*God reveals himself through **dreams and visions**.* Many followers of Jesus, and even spiritual seekers, have visions and dreams that draw them closer to God. Dreams and visions are found all through the Bible. Abraham was comforted by a vision (Gen. 15:1). The apostle Paul had a vision that directed him to a time of ministry in Macedonia (Acts 16:9). God used both Joseph and Daniel to interpret dreams (Gen. 41:1–17 and Dan. 2:28). The Lord gave Solomon a dream to set the tone and direction of his kingship (1 Kings 3:5–15). God can and does reveal himself through visions and dreams.

A dear friend of our family, Nabeel Qureshi, grew up as a devout Muslim. After years of closely examining the Christian faith and his Muslim faith, he concluded that the Bible and the gospel are true. He also realized that what he had been raised to believe as a Muslim was not founded on historical fact. He was ready to receive Jesus as God and Savior. His mind embraced the truth. But there was still a significant problem for Nabeel. His heart was holding back. His love for his family members, who were all Muslim, caused him to wait. In addition, all the years of hearing Muslim leaders declare that the Bible is untrustworthy, false, and corrupted caused lingering caution and doubts.

Nabeel came to a place where he believed in Jesus but still had some doubts in his heart. He prayed for God to give him a dream or vision about the truth of the Bible. He also prayed for courage to follow Jesus no matter what the cost might be.

God answered his prayer with a vision and three dreams. In these heavenly confirmations God assured Nabeel that the Bible is true and trustworthy. With these heavenly affirmations, Nabeel told his family and friends that he was leaving his Muslim faith and following Jesus. His story can be found in the book *Seeking Allah, Finding Jesus*. God graciously spoke and empowered Nabeel to move forward on his spiritual journey. And the vision and dreams lined right up with the teaching of the Bible.

Today our friend Nabeel is with Jesus, his Savior. After a battle with cancer, the Good Shepherd took Nabeel to his heavenly home. What started as spiritual seeking grew into a deep study of

Scripture, and over time God confirmed the truth with dreams and visions. Now Nabeel is in the very presence of the Savior who died on the cross and rose again.

Again, the real question is not, "Does God speak?" God is communicating all the time. The question we need to ask ourselves is, "Am I willing to listen and follow what God says?" That is a question we must each answer.

YOUR PRAYER JOURNEY

Over the coming week, make a point of listening for God's voice and noticing various ways the Lord is speaking. Invite God to communicate in any way he wants. As you read the Bible, pray, "Let me hear your voice as your Spirit leads me." When you go outside, ask God to let the heavens declare his glory and the earth to proclaim his creative beauty. Listen for the still, small voice of the Spirit and be ready to respond. Take note of circumstances that seem to have God's fingerprints on them. Be attentive to how God might be speaking through the people in your life. Prepare yourself in case God gives you a dream or vision that he wants to use to direct your life and speak to you. Be attentive all week long and take note of the various ways God is speaking.

Chapter Six

ARE YOU LISTENING?

*People are meant to live in an ongoing conversation
with God, speaking and being spoken to.*
—Dallas Willard, *Hearing God*

I BELIEVE THERE ARE SACRED SPACES all around us. The presence of the Holy Spirit saturates these places with a sweet holiness because the people of God have prayed deeply and consistently in these locations. It can be a living room where a family has read Scriptures, shared stories of faith, immersed themselves in intimate prayer, and shared joy that comes only through the presence of the Spirit of God. It can be the grounds of a Christian camp where children, young people, and families have worshiped with passionate voices, heard life-changing Bible messages, and met with Jesus, the Savior of the world. Church buildings, homes, even neighborhoods can become holy spaces as prayers are offered, worship is expressed, and the Word of God is read.

Kevin and I entered a space like this when we were involved in ministry with some leaders in the Chicago area. We were speaking at the Billy Graham Center for Evangelism on the campus of Wheaton College and staying in a guesthouse on the college campus called the Harbor House. The space felt holy as we entered it, and we knew that many great and godly leaders had stayed in the humble, beautiful rooms of this house through the years. Flipping through the pages of the guest book in our room revealed the names of great and saintly men and women who had stayed there. You could almost hear their prayers lingering in the air and sense the presence of Jesus in this space.

Just across the street was the Wheaton College chapel where, as a student three decades earlier, Kevin had attended worship services and student gatherings. The chapel had a bell tower across from our bedroom window. Three days into our time at the Harbor House something happened, something God used to teach me a profound lesson about prayer and listening to him.

It was nine in the morning and I was seated at a small wooden desk in a corner of our room. I was working on this book and thinking about prayer and God's love, and seeking to shape words that would help others grow in their passion and practice of prayer. Suddenly the bell rang out with clear, beautiful, and loud tones. Nine distinct times it rang—so clear it seemed impossible to ignore.

Then it struck me, like a whisper from heaven. A simple idea. A profound truth. A sobering reality. Over the past three days there had been many hours the bell had rung but I had not heard or noticed it ringing. Yet it was there—loud, clear, and undeniable. I had missed it. In my busyness, in my distracted state, in my muddled mind, preoccupied with the ordinary flow of the day, I had not noticed the ringing of the bell.

On day three of our stay on the campus of Wheaton College, it occurred to me that it was only when I was sitting quietly in my room, with my heart tuned in, that I noticed its chiming. When I silenced my mind and heart, my ears tuned in. I was finally able to hear what had been there all along.

God whispered to my heart at that moment, reminding me that he is consistently speaking to me. He never stops directing, inspiring, convicting, blessing, guiding, and talking. The problem is not that God fails to communicate with his children; the real issue is that we are distracted, busy, cluttered, and loaded down with the cares of life.

So often, our lives are an extension of my experience in the guesthouse that cool spring morning. We who know Jesus live in a sacred space, walking in the presence of the God who is always with us, omnipresent and seeking to communicate with his children. The bells are ringing. His voice is chiming. Are we quiet enough to hear and recognize his voice, the voice of the one who loves us and longs to connect with his beloved children?

If we are not careful, the ringing of those bells can even become an irritation. As we are consumed by life's demands and swept up into the frenzied pace of our modern world, the chiming can be muted. When it does cut through our distractions, we find ourselves annoyed. God's voice is there, but we see it as a disruption to our lives rather than a gift of grace.

Organic prayer isn't just about praying with our eyes wide open, it's about praying with our ears wide open too. God is speaking and seeking to communicate. The bells of his presence can be heard if we will listen. His whispers are consistent. If we will sit quietly and pay attention, we will hear from the Lover of our souls. It is time to pray with our ears open in excited anticipation, realizing that the one who spoke in the beginning and created the heavens and the earth is still speaking today.

MAKE A DECISION

As a church leader I get lots of questions about prayer. One of the most common is, "How can I learn to hear from God?" I begin by telling them how God calls us his beloved children and the sheep of his pasture. Jesus assures us that he calls us by name and leads us, and that we can recognize his voice (John 10:3–4). Hearing the voice of our Good Shepherd should be normative, not rare. In these conversations I am emphatic that Jesus will always lead us in ways that are consistent with the Bible and never contrary to the clear teaching of Scripture.

Then I invite them to decide to listen for the voice of God. Through the years I have found that most people can develop a holy habit of hearing the voice of the Shepherd if they are serious and intentional about developing this aspect of their spiritual life. Here is a process I have led many people through.

Sit, kneel, stand, lie down, or take a walk in a quiet setting. Start by finding a posture that helps you seek God. Do all you can to remove distractions. In our world today, this likely involves turning off devices that might ring, buzz, or cry out for our attention. For some of us this is a painful, and possibly unthinkable, step in the process. You may also want to have a journal or daily note card near you to write down impressions, whispers, names, convictions of sin, words of encouragement—whatever you hear. I would encourage you *not* to write down these notes in your phone or tablet, keeping those devices at a distance during this time. Despite our best efforts, our devices will quickly drive our minds toward email, social media, and countless other distractions. But it is your choice to make. Wait quietly and jot down whatever comes to your heart. Wait on the Lord. Remain quiet. Keep your heart open. Train your ears and heart to be attentive.

Invite God to speak. This might sound strange since God is always ready to speak to us. But this invitation expresses your desire to hear his voice. Tell God that you long to hear him speak. Declare that you want to be ready to follow where he leads. Throughout the Gospels, we see Jesus responding to honest desire. Commit to do all you can, with his power leading you, to follow him.

Identify the source. Generally, when we hear something in this time of waiting on God, there are three potential sources: Sovereign God, self, or Satan. Ask yourself, "Is this coming from my own mind, thoughts, family history, worry, or some other place in my heart and mind?" If it is, seek to set it aside. You can ask, "Do I have a sense that this is from the enemy? Is he seeking to confuse or mislead me?" The Scriptures are clear that the Evil One is the father of lies. In John 8:44, Jesus gives this description of the devil: "He was a murderer from the beginning, not holding to the truth, for there is no truth in him. When he lies, he speaks his native language, for he is a liar and the father of lies." If you have a sense that the Evil One is trying to mislead you, speak the name of Jesus and rebuke him. Remember what the Bible teaches: "Submit yourselves, then, to God. Resist the devil, and he will flee from you" (James 4:7). But if you have a conviction that what you are hearing is from the Lord, move to the next step.

Test it against Scripture. If the leading you are feeling lines up with the teaching of the Bible, continue to keep listening. If what you have heard is contrary to the teaching of the Bible, know that you are not hearing from God. The Holy Spirit of God will never lead a child of God to act in a way that is against what is revealed in the Bible.

Take note of God's peace. As you act on the leading of the Spirit, you should experience some measure of God's peace. Jesus said, "I have told you these things, so that in me you may have peace. In this world you will have trouble. But take heart! I have overcome the world" (John 16:33). This doesn't always mean that just because you heard from the Lord it will necessarily be easy, but I have found that there will be some measure of peace. God is Sovereign Lord over all things, and when he is present, his peace is nearby.

Get wisdom in community. God has made us for community, and asking for confirmation and wisdom from godly men and women can be very helpful. These should be people who walk closely with God and whom you trust. Listen to their wisdom and invite them into a process of praying for and with you.

Submit and obey. Once you are confident you are hearing from the Lord, and it is in line with biblical teaching, submit to the leading of the Lord and obey his promptings. Sometimes this will be a call to repentance. At other times it will be a direction for an important life decision. It could be some direction toward serving, giving, or reaching out to someone. At this point your call is to humbly obey the Lord's leading. I believe as you respond in obedience to his promptings, it opens the door to hear his voice speaking to you more clearly. Disobedience distorts our capacity to hear clearly from God. Sin deafens us to God's voice.

Learn to recognize the voice of the Good Shepherd. As you grow confident that you heard from the Lord and acted faithfully, remember how you heard from him. As time passes, you will discover that you are hearing his voice with increasing clarity and confidence. You will grow in your sensitivity to hear his voice throughout the activities of your day.

ASK GOOD QUESTIONS

Years ago my husband told me that he sometimes waits on the Lord in prayer and asks God specific questions. I had never really done this, but ever since Kevin encouraged me to try it, this has become part of my regular practice of listening for God's voice. I have discovered that specific questions will often yield very specific answers.

Some of the questions I have learned to ask God bring answers that lead to encouragement and blessing. Other questions, which are not as easy to ask, can lead to conviction and a call to repentance. I love to hear from the Lord, even when the word is one that stretches me and calls me to humble confession and repentance.

Here are some of the questions Kevin shared with me that he asks God. I would encourage you to do the same, and as you do, wait quietly and humbly for an answer.

- How much do you love me?
- In what ways are you showing me your love that I have not been paying attention to or noticing?
- In what areas of my Christian journey do you see me growing and becoming more like Jesus? How would you have me stay on this growth trajectory and go even deeper?
- Who is a person in my life that you want me to serve and show your love to in some tangible way? What would you have me do?
- Who is a person you have placed in my life that is not yet your follower but you want me to walk with them toward Jesus? What is our next step in this journey together?
- What is a hidden attitude or motive in my heart that does not honor you? How would you have me repent and change in this specific area?
- What is a pattern of continuing sin and disobedience in my life that I have become so comfortable with that it no longer bothers me? How do you feel about this sin, and what change needs to happen in my life to honor you?

- Who is one person in my family, church family, or
  neighborhood that needs a word of encouragement?

I encourage you to take time on a weekly basis to sit quietly and ask God specific questions like these, anticipating definitive answers. Since the Bible is our ultimate authority and the standard by which we judge all things, we must be people who are immersed in the Scriptures. If you are not opening the Bible on a regular basis and learning from the clear and unchanging revelation of God, I would suggest you begin there. Once this is a firm part of your spiritual growth, add a discipline of listening for the voice of the Spirit, ask great questions, and test what you hear against the truth of the Bible.

VOICE RECOGNITION

There are certain people whose voices you recognize with absolute confidence. You could hear the voice from a distance, you could have your back turned to the person, you could hear only a few words, but you would know the voice. There is no doubt.

God wants his children to recognize his voice with this level of clarity. The Good Shepherd of your soul is ready to speak in such a way that you will know when it is his voice. In the ancient world, shepherds would gather their sheep into a safe enclosure at night. Often, when there were two or more shepherds, their sheep would all share the same space. How would the shepherds separate the sheep when the sun rose and it was time for them to take their sheep out of the pen?

The answer is surprisingly simple. Each shepherd would stand by the gate of the sheep pen and call his sheep. A shepherd could speak, play a song on a flute, or even sing, and his sheep would pop their heads up, look at the shepherd, and start filing out of the enclosure. This is still the case in places of the world where multiple shepherds graze their flocks in the same area. The sheep know the voice and the song of their shepherd. In the same way, when God calls or sings to us, our heads should pop up and we should look for Jesus. Then we follow.

I don't want to make this sound too simple, but I also do not believe it needs to be overly complex. It is a journey of learning to listen and recognize the voice of our Lord, the Good Shepherd. In my own journey I have had many moments when the voice of God grew stronger and I learned to recognize it with growing clarity. One such time happened when I was a young schoolteacher in California. I loved teaching second grade and had every intention of signing my contract for another year at Ontario Christian Elementary School. But on the day I planned to sign my contract, something strange happened. I got a tickle in my throat that would not go away. Water, coughing, and throat lozenges did not help. So I asked the principal if there was any way he could find a sub for my class. I had never done this before.

A short time later I was in my VW driving on the freeway and heading home. I was amazed at how quickly they had found a sub but delighted that I would not have to struggle through the day teaching and coughing incessantly. Suddenly, like a switch being turned off, the tickle went away and the coughing stopped. I was already heading home and they already had a substitute, so I kept driving, thinking the tickle would come back, but it did not.

I have always been a rule follower, so when I got home, I went to bed. I thought this was the proper thing to do since I had told them I was sick. But as I lay there, I did not feel sick at all, and I was not tired. Instead, something else happened. Over the next few hours God began speaking to me. And the whole trajectory of my life changed!

The only way I can describe what happened is that I began to wrestle with God in prayer. Like Jacob, I spoke with God and he spoke back to me. We wrestled and he won . . . he always does!

My plan at that time was to keep teaching as Kevin went through seminary and finished his master of divinity degree. I had thought about getting a master of education after Kevin had a job as a pastor, but at this point in our lives, I was our primary source of income. Kevin worked full time at a church, but the pay was modest and we could not make it without my income.

As I lay in bed, pondering how well I felt and wondering why the tickle had come so fiercely and gone away so quickly, God spoke. I heard with my spiritual ears, not my physical ears, but the message was crystal clear. I recognized God's voice: "Don't sign your teaching contract. Go to seminary with Kevin."

In this moment, as in many moments in my life, I knew God was speaking because I responded and entered the conversation. "Lord, I am the family income, I can't stop teaching. We will have no money to pay our rent and bills." The message from the Lord remained. We wrestled on. I explained to God that I had taken one theology class in my undergraduate work, and it stretched and challenged me more than any other class. When I finished that class, I breathed a sigh of relief and said, "I will never have to take another theology class again!" Of course, God knew all of this, but I told him anyway. We wrestled on.

I felt a growing conviction that I needed to stop teaching and get a degree in theology. It did not make sense, but I recognized the voice of my Good Shepherd and continued to talk with him about my "concerns." Eventually God took a firmer tone, asking me, "Do you want to be in my will?" I humbly responded, "Yes, Lord, I want to be in your will." He affirmed what I had heard earlier, "Then go to seminary." A measure of peace came over me. I knew what I had to do. I was unsure how we would make it and what people would think of my decision, but I knew I could not sign my contract and return to teaching.

At this point, I contacted a few trusted people and shared what I believed God was speaking into my life. As I received counsel from other wise Christians (including my parents) over the next couple of hours, I received affirmation. Even my principal, who really appreciated having me on his teaching staff, said that my decision did not surprise him at all, and he believed it was the right thing for me to do.

Before the day was over, I had met with an administrator at the seminary Kevin was attending and discovered they had a "Team Ministry Grant" that covered 75 percent of the tuition for the spouse of a married couple attending seminary together. I would go on in the coming term to pursue a master's in their school of theology with an emphasis on Christian formation and discipleship.

As I look back on those years, I remember how much they stretched me. I also recall that season with great fondness. I am thankful I heard the Shepherd's call and followed.

HINDRANCES TO HEARING GOD

God is speaking. But are we listening? If God speaks with clarity, why don't we hear him more often? Why don't we respond with greater confidence? In the same way that there are conditions that help us hear God's whispers and words more clearly, there are also things that keep us from hearing God. These need to be identified and overcome if we want to pray with our eyes and ears wide open.

Unbelief. Prayer is not a magic incantation designed to get what we want from God. It is a conversation in the context of a relationship, an encounter with God. If we do not believe in God and have not met his Son, Jesus Christ, we have not entered this relationship. If we don't trust God to speak and refuse to believe that he still is interacting with his children, it is very unlikely we will hear his voice, even when he shouts.

We counter this obstacle by entering and developing a personal relationship with God through faith in Jesus. When we trust that the Good Shepherd still speaks and his sheep can and should recognize his voice, we find that we can better listen to and hear from him.

Mental clutter. Have you ever had a hard time finding an article of clothing in a closet packed so full of random stuff that it is hard to close the door? Sometimes our minds and hearts can be cluttered with worry, fear, and even bad theology. This makes it harder to hear when the Holy Spirit is whispering or speaking.

If we want to hear God more clearly, we need to unclutter our minds by filling them with Scripture. This will help drive worry and fear away. The truth of God's Word helps us order our lives and thoughts around the things that honor him.

Busyness. The faster we move, the harder it is to hear. If you are in a car driving 70 mph past someone standing on the sidewalk trying to talk with you, it is unlikely you will hear anything that person says as you go screaming by. If you are riding a bike past someone trying to tell you something, you might pick up a few random words—maybe even a whole sentence. If you are walking by the person, you will hear quite a bit more. If you stop, face the person, and give your full attention, you will hear everything that person says. Our pace affects how well we can hear when someone is speaking to us. This is true with every relationship, whether it is with a spouse, a child, a friend, or even God. There is something about the hurried pace of a busy heart and life that makes listening more difficult.

As we learn to slow down, to be quiet, and to listen, we hear God more clearly. This means adjusting the pace of our daily schedule and the flow of our week. I am convinced that one of the reasons God calls his children to slow down one day a week and enjoy the gift of a Sabbath is that he knows we need to hear from him and our busy lives can get in the way. As fewer Christians have a rhythm of weekly Sabbath rest, fewer people seem to hear from God. I encourage you to make a point of setting up a time of quiet in the flow of each day to meet with God and listen to him. In addition, you would be wise to develop a pattern of Sabbath each week when you dial back your pace and find a place of rest in God.

Negative view of self. "Why would God speak to me?" "I am not good enough to hear from God." Many people today have decided that God will not speak to them directly. "God might speak to a pastor, priest, or church leader, but not to someone like me." If we think this way, we will likely miss the wonderful things God is saying to us.

The antidote to this sickness of mind is the truth we have already discussed. We are God's precious creation, we are the sheep of his pasture, and we are his beloved children. When we see ourselves through the eyes of God, we realize that he wants to speak to us, his sons and daughters.

Untrained ears. Many people have simply never learned to hear and recognize the voice of the Good Shepherd. Their ears are untrained. By using the simple process discussed in this chapter and developing your hearing, you can learn to recognize the voice of your heavenly Father.

A sinful lifestyle. When we are living in open rebellion to God and brazen disobedience to his Word, our ears can become deaf to his voice. It is not that God stops speaking; it is that we are simply unable to hear. When the Holy Spirit has convicted us over and over and we have persistently ignored his promptings, we learn to block out God's heavenly voice. When we are perfectly aware that we are living in opposition to the will of God and we don't care, it becomes hard to hear new and fresh words from God.

Confession and repentance are the only way to overcome the hindrance of a sinful lifestyle. We must identify our sin and tell God we are sorry. We also need to repent and change our behavior, attitude, and choices. Being sorry is not enough. We need to be changed! When we turn from our sin and follow the teaching of Scripture and the conviction of the Holy Spirit, our ears are open and tuned in to hear from our Lord.

———

God is speaking. More than we imagine, God is seeking to connect with us each day. We need to listen. We need to hear from God and remove the hindrances that stand in the way. God is not only speaking but also listening for us to engage with him. When this happens, we enter into two-way conversation with the Maker and Ruler of the universe.

YOUR PRAYER JOURNEY

Over the coming week, try three exercises that will tune your ears to the voice of God, who is always speaking. First, make a decision that you want to hear God with greater clarity. Use the process in this chapter that begins with coming before God quietly in a posture that fits what is happening in your heart. Move through the process and see if it helps you tune your heart to the heart of God and open your ears to whatever way he wants to speak to you. Second, take time to ask God specific questions, and wait quietly and expectantly for answers. You might want to have something to write with so you can collect thoughts that God places on your heart and speaks to you. You can use the questions from this chapter or come up with your own. The key is patience as you listen. And always weigh what you hear against the teaching of the Bible. Finally, take time to pray through the hindrances listed in this chapter. Are any of these getting in the way of your hearing from the Lord? If the Holy Spirit convicts you that there is something standing between you and the Lord who loves you, deal with this hindrance with humility and tenacity.

Chapter Seven

GOD IS LISTENING, ARE YOU SPEAKING?

*One great reason for prayerlessness is the lack of
the living, joyous assurance that God will hear us. But if
God's servant gets a vision of the living God waiting to
grant their request, and to bestow all the heavenly gifts of
the Spirit they are in need of, for themselves or those they
are serving, how everything would be set aside to make
time and room for this wonderful power that ensures
heavenly blessing—the power of faith!*
—Andrew Murray

CONTRARY TO POPULAR OPINION, prayer is not primarily about getting what we want from God. It is about entering into God's plan for us. Prayer is not about getting ahold of God, it is about the Lord of the universe getting ahold of us. I learned this lesson in a powerful way while sitting on the sidelines of a soccer game, cheering on my son.

There I sat, with all the other soccer moms and dads on the sidelines. It was a sunny Michigan day, and I was ready to fully engage in support of my son, even to pray for him. I prayed with my eyes wide open, intently watching my son and his teammates as they warmed up for the game. "Lord, help my son's team to win. They have practiced so hard, and a win would be such an encouragement to them. In the name of Jesus, amen."

As I was praying, my eyes fell on the line of soccer moms and dads on the other side of the field. These were the parents of the kids playing on the opposing team. As I looked more closely at these parents, I recognized a number of them. They attended our church!

Even as I was praying for our team to be victorious, it hit me— these other parents were probably praying the same thing. They, too, wanted their children to have a great day, score some goals, and experience the affirmation of winning. As parents on opposite sides of the field, might we be putting God in a bit of a conundrum? What is the Lord of glory to do when parents from the same church, who all love their children and all believe in the power of prayer, pray in direct opposition to each other?

To this point in my day, my prayers had been a monologue, letting God know what I would like from him. When this dilemma hit me, I shifted to a dialogue in my prayer. Instead of telling God to grant our team victory, I asked God, *What should I pray?* I wondered what Jesus would pray if he were in such a situation.

I thought of Jesus' teaching in the gospel of John when he said, "And I will do whatever you ask in my name, so that the Father may be glorified in the Son. You may ask me for anything in my name, and I will do it" (John 14:13–14). Does this verse promise that I will get whatever I want as long as I ask in prayer and give a hearty "In the name of Jesus" at the end of my supplication? What if two Christians are asking for opposing things? Does God become the great heavenly tiebreaker? Or is there more to prayer than my simply getting what I ask?

The kids were stretching and the game had not even started and already my head was spinning with theological quandaries. "Lord, is it wrong to pray for my son's team to win?" I had a conviction in my heart that it was not wrong, in a sinful way, to pray this, but I also felt there might be better ways to pray. I asked the Lord, "Teach me to pray. Show me how to communicate with you in situations like this. I want to be a person of prayer, but I suspect that sometimes my prayers are too narrow and self-serving."

The Holy Spirit responded. He flooded my mind and heart with new ways to pray. Instead of simply asking for a victory for half the kids on the field, why not pray for all the children to play to the best of their abilities? Why not pray for each player to have fun and stay safe and injury free? This would allow me to pray for each child, no matter the color of the jersey. I began to pray in this way, moving my eyes from child to child. By now the game had started, so I prayed for these athletes as they ran, kicked, dove, and sometimes fell down. I felt the Lord prompting me to pray for each child who knew Jesus to grow in Christlikeness, whether they won or lost, and for the Christian players and parents (including me) to be positive witnesses for those who did not yet know Jesus.

By the time the game was over, I had learned a new way of talking to the God who listens. And I discovered more about listening to the God who speaks. I can't even remember if my son's team won that game, but I will never forget what I learned about speaking to God that day. No matter how the game turned out, the day was a win—every child received the blessing of prayer.

God really is listening, and he wants us to speak to him. He loves when his children communicate with their heavenly Father. The problem is that our prayers are often too small. We ask for victories at sporting events, we request toys that break and rust, and we cry out for transitory pleasures.

When we read what Jesus said in John 14:13–14, "And I will do whatever you ask in my name, so that the Father may be glorified in the Son. You may ask me for anything in my name, and I will do it," we often rush to the "ask me for anything" and miss the heart of Jesus' words. What if the purpose behind this invitation is Jesus trying to teach us how to speak intimately and effectively with God? What if this passage is about more than getting answers to our requests for things we want? What is Jesus getting at in this often-quoted and rarely understood passage?

THREE LESSONS ABOUT SPEAKING TO GOD

Let's start with the broader context of Jesus' words in John 14. Although there are seven more chapters in the gospel, we are drawing near to the close of Jesus' life and ministry. The cross is looming and the end is near. Jesus taught in the upper room, he instituted the sacrament of Communion, and he washed the disciples' feet. Shortly after this he lifted up what is often called his High Priestly Prayer and gave his final detailed instructions to his followers before going to the cross to pay for our sins.

When Jesus teaches about prayer in John 14:12–14, we should tune in and prepare to learn. His words are bold and epic, with promises almost too big to believe. Jesus says we will do the kinds of works he has been doing, we will do greater things than what he had done, and we can ask for anything in his name and he will do it. This sounds like a blank check—an absolute promise. But when we look closer, we understand that in context God is inviting us to speak, listen, and trust his wisdom. What is Jesus teaching us about speaking to the God who is always listening?

God invites us to ask. Since God is listening, he is ever ready to hear our prayers and receive our requests. But God is not a Santa Claus figure who waits once a year for the list of presents we want. He is not a heavenly Buddha whose belly we rub for good luck to get what we want. He is not our lucky rabbit's foot that we keep in our pocket and take out when we need a little heavenly magic. James is painfully clear when he writes, "When you ask, you do not receive, because you ask with wrong motives, that you may spend what you get on your pleasures" (4:3). God wants us to ask, but he is not raising spoiled children who demand whatever they want and pout if they don't get their requests in the right size, style, or time.

Instead, we are to ask with humility and wisdom. God wants to hear our desires and passions, but he delights when these are being shaped and formed by his presence in our lives and his will for the world around us.

We are to do this in the name of Jesus. After assuring us that God wants us to ask of him, we are instructed to pray in the name of Jesus. For so many of us, all this means is tagging the words "In the name of Jesus" on the end of our prayer. If our theology is unbiblical, we might treat these words like a magic incantation that we believe assures us we will get what we want from God. Is that what Jesus is teaching his people right before he goes to the cross and dies in our place for our sins?

There is much more going on here. When Jesus calls us to pray in his name, he is calling us to pray *as he would pray.* When an ambassador represents a country and speaks in its name, this person stands as a representative of that nation. They are to speak only what is consistent with the will of the sovereign states they represent. Ambassadors do not say whatever they want and place the weight of a country behind their words. Instead, they are to faithfully represent the names and wills of their countries. In the same way, when we pray in the name of Jesus, we are declaring that our prayer is consistent with the heart of Jesus and the will of the Father.

Our requests and the fruit of our prayers are meant to bring glory to the Father. When we ask with humility and wisdom, and when we pray consistently with the heart of our Savior, the third part of Jesus' teaching follows naturally. Our prayers will bring glory to the Father. When we pray, we should always be asking the question, "Will this bring praise and honor to the God who saved me?" Will this prayer, if answered in the affirmative, lift up God and glorify his holy name?

LORD, TEACH US TO PRAY

One day Jesus was with his followers and he was praying. One of his disciples made a beautiful and wise request: "Lord, teach us to pray" (Luke 11:1). In this setting, and in Luke's gospel, Jesus gives them a simple version of a prayer he taught many times and in many settings:

> Father,
> hallowed be your name,
> your kingdom come.
> Give us each day our daily bread.
> Forgive us our sins,
>> for we also forgive everyone who sins against us.
> And lead us not into temptation.

—Luke 11:2–4

Look at this brief but potent prayer. It reinforces the same three things Jesus taught in John 14. Line by line we see the invitation to ask. But the asking is wise, and it is not about petty and self-centered things. Each line reflects the heart of Jesus and affirms his will. And each request, if it were answered in the affirmative, would give glory to the God of heaven.

SPEAKING TO THE GOD WHO IS LISTENING

My aunt Zelma was a wonderful woman of God who influenced my faith through my childhood and into my adult years. She outlived her husband and two of her three sons, but her faith only seemed to grow stronger with each passing year and every tragedy she weathered.

One day my phone rang and my mother let me know that Aunt Zelma was drawing near the end of her life. She would be moving to a hospice center a few miles from my home, which meant she would be farther from my mom but closer to me. I had a clear sense in my heart that God was giving me the honor of caring for a dear family member who had served so many others throughout her life.

When I got off the phone, I whispered this prayer: "God, I am available. I would love to minister to my aunt in her last days." In moments like these I sometimes raise a hand, like a little girl in a school class, as if to say, "Teacher, choose me!" I let God know I was up for whatever he wanted to bring my way.

Soon afterward I went to the hospice center to see Aunt Zelma, but the caregivers were fully engaged with her. It was clearly a bad time for a visit, so I slipped out without being noticed and decided to come back another time soon. The second time I came, she was not in her room, so again I left and committed to try again. The third time was, sadly, not the charm either. When I came to her room, her pastor was with her, working on the details of her funeral. It was clearly inappropriate for me to barge in on their time together. Strike three.

As I walked out of the hospice center, I began to pray: "God, I can't believe how bad my timing has been. I really want to be present for Aunt Zelma. Could you please help me? You know my heart, Lord. I don't want her to be alone in these last days." I didn't think much about my prayer, because short little prayers as I walk through life are now a normal part of my day.

A few days later, at about 4:30 in the afternoon, I was picking up some clothes from the dry cleaner. As I was standing in line, I felt the Holy Spirit nudge me to go visit my aunt. I dismissed the thought because I really needed to get home to start dinner. But the stirring continued, and the Lord brought to my memory the prayer I had lifted to him just a few days before. Could this be God's Spirit answering my request to be used by him in these last days of my aunt Zelma's life?

I called Kevin as I left the dry cleaner and shared what was happening. He encouraged me to go visit her. As I walked in and introduced myself to the woman at the front desk, she quickly let me know that the timing of my arrival was perfect. My aunt's only living son had been there earlier that day but had left a short time before, and Zelma had just taken a significant turn for the worse. She was drawing near the end. They had been trying to reach her son, but to no avail.

When I entered her room, I found my precious aunt with a sweet hospice nurse by her side. I took the seat on the other side of the bed. She was coherent but struggling a bit. My aunt breathed a sigh of relief to have me by her side, and I assured her I would not leave. I sat quietly, read some psalms with her permission, and softly sang a few hymns. It was obvious her time to leave and be with Jesus was drawing near.

As we entered a third hour of being together, I prayed a simple prayer in my heart asking God to direct me as I sought more passages that would be appropriate to read to her. I waited quietly and felt a clear prompting to read Psalm 27, knowing how much that passage has ministered to me in the past. I began reading,

> The LORD is my light and my salvation—
> whom shall I fear?
> The LORD is the stronghold of my life—
> of whom shall I be afraid?
>
> —verses 1–2

As I finished the second verse, I glanced up and looked into her eyes. I could sense God's presence in the room. It was palpable. I reassured her that the Lord was with her, and in that moment she slipped away into the arms of her Savior. The Good Shepherd came, took his precious lamb on his shoulders, and brought her to green pastures.

As I walked out of the hospice center that night, I couldn't help but reflect on God's graciousness in hearing my prayer. The God who listens knew my heartfelt longing that Zelma would be with loved ones at the end of her life. The God who speaks alerted me to the exact time she needed me to be there. On three occasions, my timing was not right. This time I responded to God's prompting and his timing was perfect.

While sitting at her funeral a few days later, her pastor stood up and began to share that it was hard to pick just a couple of passages for the service because Zelma had so many favorites. Then he said, "I do know one passage that was particularly meaningful for Zelma. It was Psalm 27." He opened his Bible and began to read:

> The LORD is my light and my salvation—
> whom shall I fear?
> The LORD is the stronghold of my life—
> of whom shall I be afraid?

These were the exact same words Zelma had heard me read to her as she slipped from this life and entered her heavenly home.

Praying throughout our day anywhere, at any time, and in any circumstance will lead to experiences that honor God and bless those around us. Talking to God in two-way communication leads to moments when we see God responding to our heart's cry to be a servant who honors him. Speaking to the God who listens and listening to the God who speaks makes every day an adventure. It leads to sacred moments when God shows up and heaven intersects with earth in beautiful ways.

YOUR PRAYER JOURNEY

Each time you pray in the coming week, begin by saying, "Lord, I want my prayer to be in the name of Jesus. Please let all I pray be motivated by Jesus, consistent with the heart of Jesus, and for the glory of Jesus." If you are not confident your prayer reflects the will and desire of Jesus, slow down and ask yourself if you should be praying in this way. If you are confident your prayer is consistent with the desires of the Savior and honors your heavenly Father, when you finish your prayer, speak these words with authority and confidence: "In the name of Jesus, amen!"

Chapter Eight

HOLY CONVERSATIONS

*To be with God, there is no need to be continually
in church. We may make an oratory of our heart
wherein to retire from time to time to converse with Him
in meekness, humility and love. There is not in the world
a kind of life more sweet and delightful than that of a
continual conversation with God.*

—Brother Lawrence

IT WAS OUR ONE-YEAR ANNIVERSARY, and Kevin's parents
had kindly given us a dinner out and a night away at a local hotel.
At that time in our lives, we were beyond broke, so this was a big
deal for us. We never ate out at nice restaurants—they were far too
expensive. We never went to hotels—there was no reason for it.
So this was a special time. I should have been happy and content.
Instead, I was frustrated with my husband.

There was something I had been noticing for more than a year
now. I had trouble articulating my frustration, but things came to
the surface on that morning in our hotel room. We had both taken

some time to read our Bibles and pray. As we had done so many times before, we talked about what we learned from the Scriptures. While sharing, Kevin mentioned that while he was praying, the Holy Spirit had spoken to him and put a number of things on his heart.

That was when I started feeling agitated. Kevin would talk about prayer as if it were a conversation with God. He acted like he heard from God as he would hear from a friend. And honestly, it bugged me. I had never said anything to him before, but this day it just came out.

"Kevin, you often share things God speaks to you. I know we can talk to God, and I am confident he hears us. But I don't hear God speaking to me, at least not like you describe it."

Kevin went on to explain that his prayers often included speaking and listening. Holy conversations. Familiar but sacred at the same time. He told me he recognized God's voice like he recognized the voices of his parents and friends and even my voice.

Honestly, this didn't help with my frustration. I said to him, "I have been a Christian since I was five years old. I believe the Bible. I love Jesus. I pray a lot, but I don't hear God speaking to me in a voice I recognize."

My husband, who was not known for his sensitivity in our early years of marriage (and he would agree with me on this), looked at me and said words that hurt and challenged me at the same time: "If you don't hear God speaking to you and if you don't recognize his voice, I believe that is your fault."

I looked at him, not sure how to respond. I asked him to explain. "What do you mean it's my fault?" He went on to ask me a series of questions. "Do you expect to hear from God? Do you ask questions of God and wait for answers? Have you sought to recognize his voice? Do you believe that God still speaks to his children?"

His questions launched me on a spiritual quest. In that moment, the truth of God's Scriptures cascaded over my heart reminding me that God loves all his children. If he would speak to Kevin, wouldn't he also speak to me? What good parent speaks to one child but not to another? Maybe God was speaking but I was just not noticing and responding.

Instead of growing frustrated and resentful, I was moved to deeper places of prayer than I had experienced before. I began waiting quietly on the Holy Spirit. I started asking God questions and expecting my heavenly Father to answer. And over the next year my spiritual life grew and changed. I found myself engaged in holy conversations where I would speak to God and listen for his voice. Within a couple of years I found myself conversing with God, sometimes with eyes wide open, at many times and in many places during my day. I even had a prayer chair at our home in Michigan, and at times I would hear the Holy Spirit whisper, "Go to your prayer chair, be still, I want to speak with you." This became a normative and common part of my walk with Jesus.

THE "WHERE" OF HOLY CONVERSATIONS

The beauty of organic prayer is that you can converse with God anywhere and anytime. Although I have a chair where I love to sit and talk with Jesus, the vast majority of my prayer time is not in the quiet of the morning sitting in my chair. My holy conversations happen in stores and restaurants, during drives, on hikes, and even in places that don't seem "holy" at first glance. Ordinary and secular places become sacred when we engage in holy conversations.

I have a friend who is a medical doctor. He prays before every surgery and procedure he does. If the patient makes the request, he will pray with the patient in the operating room in the presence of the anesthesiologist and nursing staff. In these situations, he prays out loud. At other times, his dialogue with God is done quietly in his heart. He is speaking and listening as he does his work throughout the day.

In case you are wondering, this doctor works in a very secular setting, not a Christian hospital. But he would tell you that he can't do his job to the best of his ability without speaking to God and listening for the wisdom and leading of the Holy Spirit.

I'VE GOT THIS!

I knew Rod for two and a half decades. He grew up going to church. His Christian faith was genuine. He read his Bible, prayed, and tried to let his relationship with Jesus influence his life. Those who knew him well also knew he had times when he struggled with intimacy with God. When Rod became part of our family, I liked him immediately. He was a gentle and unassuming man with a warm smile and a kind disposition. He was also a wonderful father to my niece and nephew.

When we received word that he had cancer, it was a blow to our whole family. When the cancer advanced to the point where only a miracle would save him, we were deeply concerned. We were also praying for our niece and nephew, Kristin and Matt, because we knew the loss of their dad would be very painful.

In November of that year Rod contacted me because he had heard that Kevin and I would be in Michigan a short time before he was scheduled for a complex brain surgery. He wanted to meet with some family members and most important with the kids. True to his character over all the years we knew him, he was not concerned about himself. He was mostly concerned for Kristin and Matt, as there was a high probability that they would be moving into the adult years of their life without him. He was selfless, all the way to the end.

During that family gathering, Rod shared what I call his "burning bush" moment. The reality of his situation had hit him especially hard. He knew that his life might be drawing to a close. The doctors had made it clear the cancer was widespread and advanced. He told us of a day, several weeks earlier, when he was driving in his truck and God showed up. Rod's eyes were open and so were his ears, and like Moses hearing God speak words of comfort and hope, Rod knew the Lord was speaking to him that day. "I was driving my truck down the road and getting ready to turn on 112th Street. I was feeling the weight of not being there for Kristin and Matt. Then it happened. I heard God speak. With absolute clarity I heard the words, *'I've got this!'*"

He went on to explain that he had heard people talk about God speaking to them, but he never really understood what they meant. He never fully believed what they were claiming. "Now I know it's true," he said. "I know people hear from God. I have experienced the presence of God." From that day onward we all saw a noticeable difference in Rod's walk with Jesus. We could see on his face and hear in his voice that he was a different person after this encounter with the Living God.

For most of his life, Rod had spoken to God in prayer. Now he had heard God speak to him, and it brought him great joy. His life changed, his faith grew deeper, and his prayers became more personal than ever before. He continued to battle cancer, giving all he could to fight this dreadful disease. He spent time with Kristin and Matt and the rest of his family. About four months later, on

March 28 of that year, Rod met the one who had whispered in his ears as he drove down the road. This time, instead of saying, "I've got this," I suspect God said, "I've got you."

THE "WHAT" OF HOLY CONVERSATIONS

All holy conversation begins with the God of the universe.

God speaks, we hear. Often we think that we are the initiators, but God is the sovereign ruler of all things. If he had not reached out to us first, we would never be able to find him. One of the joys of this reality is that God tends to speak in ways we can understand. For Rod, the words "I've got this" were perfect, just what Rod needed to hear. We should expect God to speak in ways we will understand. We should keep our ears open to anything God wants to say. When the prophet Eli taught little Samuel to pray, he instructed him to say, "Speak, Lord, for your servant is listening" (1 Sam. 3:9). We would do well to pray in the same way.

We speak, God hears. Once we hear from God, we need to respond. If you hear a word of conviction from the Holy Spirit, respond with confession. Or ask, "What would you have me do? How should I change? How can I live differently and honor you?" Then listen for an answer. If you hear a word of blessing and encouragement from the Lord, thank him and ask for power to live more fully for his glory. Over and over we are assured that if we pray to God, he hears us (1 John 5:14; Ps. 66:17–20). This interplay of hearing and speaking can go back and forth many times, like any other conversation.

We obey, God is glorified. As God speaks to us and we respond, this should lead to life-transforming action. In the book of James, we are told that we are not to simply hear the word of the Lord, but we are to be moved to action (James 1:22). Part of holy conversation is heart and life change. Our holy conversations with God should shape our attitudes, change our motives, launch us outward with compassionate action, drive us to our knees in confession, shape our character. Holy conversations lead to holy living.

GO TO THE ENDS OF THE EARTH

I experienced this exact process when the leader of the board for a nonprofit named World Mission said to me, "I really would like to see one of our board members join the team that will be doing our largest solar audio Bible distribution so far." As a member of the board, I knew how important this trip was, but in my mind I did not think it was the right trip for me to go on. It involved hand delivering what are called Treasures (audio Bibles) to remote people living in small villages in the Himalayas. The trip would include long flights and rigorous living conditions, and not a single woman had signed up for the portion of the trip they were asking me to join. We would be trekking the Himalayas for five days.

My dilemma was that I felt a strong conviction of the Holy Spirit as I walked out of that board meeting. I felt that I was supposed to go on this trip. I knew God was speaking because I responded—I began to explain to God why I should not go. Over the years I have found that I often know God is talking to me because I notice I am talking back. This is usually a sign that I need to step back and listen more closely.

I began to reason with God. I would be the only woman on this portion of the trip and Kevin was already committed to lead another mission trip, so he would be unable to accompany me.

I had also gone through a complex neck surgery and was still in physical therapy and in a healing process. I listed all my objections to God as I tried to negotiate my way out of going.

Of course, God did not let up. The conviction and whispers continued for some time. The sense that I should go with the team to India and Nepal only grew stronger. I spoke to God: "Lord, I am willing to go if this is your will. But I feel it would not be right for me to be the only woman on the trip and not have my husband there. Lord, open a door or change my heart."

A short time after that specific prayer, God answered. I was telling our oldest son, Zach, about the challenge I was facing. I explained my concerns and asked him to pray for me. He responded with a question, "What if I go with you and the team?" A wave of Spirit-given peace came over me. I felt this was God's answer. I was to go on the trip—with my son.

God spoke and I listened. I spoke and God heard my concerns. God spoke and continued to call me. I expressed my reasons why it would not work. God provided a way. We had gone back and forth a number of times over several weeks before the answer finally came.

I went on the trip with the team *and* with my son. God was present and we saw pastors receive amazing resources, we shared the gospel, and we handed out hundreds of audio Bibles in the native languages that were represented. We watched as lives were changed for eternity. Zach and I were obedient to the call and God was glorified. The experience of trekking the Himalayas with the World Mission team and my son was powerful in its own way. We hiked for six hours each day, sleeping in unheated huts and at times using bathroom facilities that were essentially holes in the ground. That trip proved to be one of the best experiences of my life. Only God! I am so thankful I listened and followed his voice.

This is holy conversation at its best. Always real, often messy, time-consuming, and life-changing!

THE ULTIMATE HOLY CONVERSATION

In the very beginning of the book of Hebrews, we discover what I now call the "Ultimate Holy Conversation." Read these words slowly and let their power penetrate your soul: "In the past God spoke to our ancestors through the prophets at many times and in various ways, but in these last days he has spoken to us by his Son, whom he appointed heir of all things, and through whom also he made the universe. The Son is the radiance of God's glory and the exact representation of his being, sustaining all things by his powerful word. After he had provided purification for sins, he sat down at the right hand of the Majesty in heaven" (Heb. 1:1–3).

God has spoken with clarity and power through his prophets. The Scriptures are the absolute and final revelation of God: unchanging, true, and Spirit-breathed. But in these last days, God has spoken to us through Jesus, the Christ, his only Son.

The ultimate conversation we can have with God is the gospel. It is the good news of Jesus Christ. The God of heaven has spoken through his only begotten Son, and the message is clear: "But God demonstrates his own love for us in this: While we were still sinners, Christ died for us" (Rom. 5:8). Though we were lost in sin and condemned to death, God offered life through the sacrifice of Jesus, the Lamb of God who takes away the sins of the world (Rom. 3:23; 6:23; John 1:29). Jesus, the Word of God, has spoken: "Come to me." We respond to his grace by faith alone and say, "Yes, Lord, I come" (Rom. 10:9–10). When we confess our sins and declare our trust in him, we are cleansed (1 John 1:9).

This is the ultimate holy conversation. God calls our name and offers us his grace. We confess our sins and declare our faith. When this happens, a lost lamb is found (Luke 15:3–7), a wandering child comes home (Luke 15:11–27), and the angels of heaven rejoice (Luke 15:10). After this first conversation, the door is opened to us and we have full access to our Father through the work of Jesus as the Holy Spirit leads us. We can talk to God and begin a lifetime of holy conversations.

SHARING WHAT WE HAVE RECEIVED

Some years ago Kevin and I were in Alaska training a group of leaders how to share their faith in natural ways through our ministry, Organic Outreach. At dinner, one of the leaders told us that she felt bad that we had not been able to see the northern lights (the aurora borealis) during our visit. She asked another person at the table, who happened to be a gifted photographer, if he had any of his pictures of the aurora borealis on his phone, and he did. As I looked at these strangely beautiful pictures, my first thought was that I wished my parents could see them. I had a glimpse of their beauty and immediately wanted others to experience it.

There is a powerful theological truth here: when we encounter something meaningful, we immediately want others to share in this experience.

As Kevin and I have trained leaders and congregations around the world over the past three decades, we have met many Christians who love Jesus but do not feel they are ready to share their faith with others. They pray passionately but do not believe they are equipped to tell the story of Jesus to people who do not yet follow the Savior. But what the Bible teaches is dramatically different!

While equipping and teaching are helpful, the truth is that from the moment we receive the grace of Jesus and become his children, we can pray for others and begin to share the life-changing message of the Savior.

As God reaches out to us and lifts us from the pit of our sin and gives us new life, we are called to reach out to others as well. "Therefore, if anyone is in Christ, the new creation has come: The old has gone, the new is here! All this is from God, who reconciled us to himself through Christ and gave us the ministry of reconciliation" (2 Cor. 5:17–18). There is no sense that this new follower of Jesus needs years of training or a series of classes to prepare them to pass on what they have received. They can begin immediately, and many do, with great impact for the kingdom. Of course, training and equipping are absolutely valuable and should be encouraged. But the moment a person comes to faith in Jesus, they are his ambassador and can begin passing on their faith to others.

One of my ministry responsibilities at Shoreline Church is building a team of people who will meet one-on-one with new believers and help them take first steps of faith. It is a joy when I get to meet with people who have accepted the grace of Jesus and are starting their journey of faith. I've found there is one recurring thing that happens that assures me they really get what is going on in their life. It has happened over and over through the years.

I will meet with a brand-new Christian and they will look at me and say something like, "I have to tell my dad about Jesus," or "I am bringing my little brother to church so he can learn about God's love," or "I am telling all my friends at school about Jesus." I realize they get it! At the same moment they become part of God's family, they want to reach out and help others meet the Savior who has changed their life and eternity.

THE REST OF THE STORY

As we began this chapter, I told you about my first anniversary and how I was irritated with my husband because I did not have what he had. Kevin had been a Christian for only six years while I had loved Jesus for almost two decades. I resented the fact that he seemed to have this close personal connection with God in prayer that I had missed.

We sat in that hotel room working through a theology of prayer and communication with God. I asked Kevin how he began entering into conversational prayer. His answer was simple and even humorous: "Before I became a Christian, I watched and listened to the people around me who were living for Jesus. They talked about Jesus like they knew him, like he was a friend, like Jesus actually loved them."

Then Kevin looked straight at me and said, "I believed them! So, when I received the grace of Jesus and his sacrifice on the cross, I just started praying to Jesus like a friend. I assumed a friend would not leave you hanging but would respond. And Jesus did respond. He still does, every day."

Now Kevin and I journey through life together, praying with our eyes and ears wide open. It is not unusual for us to pray together five to ten times a day. We rarely stop what we are doing and say, "Let's pray." We close our eyes sometimes. But most of the time one of us just begins praying as we walk, talk, drive, eat, and do life together. Our conversations with each other are infused with prayer. And those prayers are holy conversations.

Some of you reading this chapter might feel discouraged just like I did on my first anniversary. Maybe you really want to hear from God, but you are not feeling connected in a way that allows you to recognize his voice. Don't be disheartened. Keep praying, listening, and responding when God speaks through the Bible, through people, and through circumstances. Be faithful when God does speak and keep listening. Remove mental clutter, ask God good questions, and be patient. God is ready to speak, but it will be in his timing.

YOUR PRAYER JOURNEY

Holy conversations are not complete until we take action on what God has spoken to us. God does speak. We respond to him. Humble obedience is the fruit of our holy conversations. Take time and reflect on some of the ways God has clearly spoken to you but you have not taken action. It could be a conversation where the Holy Spirit convicted you of sin, but you have still not repented and turned from a specific attitude or behavior. It could be a conversation when God called you to begin serving, giving more generously, or sharing your faith more boldly. You have heard from God, but you have not yet responded. When you identify a way God has spoken and you have not yet acted, commit to obedient submission. Pray for power. Tell a Christian friend what you plan to do so you have accountability. Confess to God that you have been holding back, and invite your heavenly Father to move you forward in action that puts hands and feet to your prayers.

Part Three

PRAYING WITH HEARTS WIDE OPEN

*I pray that the eyes of your heart may be enlightened in
order that you may know the hope to which he has called
you, the riches of his glorious inheritance in his holy
people, and his incomparably great power for us who
believe. That power is the same as the mighty strength he
exerted when he raised Christ from the dead and seated
him at his right hand in the heavenly realms.*

—Ephesians 1:18–20 (emphasis added)

A HEART OPEN to God will help you see who he is and pray with
greater passion and transparent honesty. A heart tuned in to God
will alert you to the spiritual battles Christians face in our world
today and lead you to victory over the enemy. When we open our
hearts to God in prayer, his peace fills us and anxiety scurries away,
running for the back door.

Chapter Nine

THE FATHER IS FOND OF YOU

*This is love: not that we loved God, but that he loved
us and sent his Son as an atoning sacrifice for our sins.*
—1 John 4:10

OVER A LIFETIME of processing data and learning, some lessons, some pieces of simple information can be missed. Important truths get passed over and never settle into our full awareness. My husband, Kevin, is a bright man and a serious student. When we were married, he had already graduated from college and was working on his master's degree. But there were still some strange gaps in his education and knowledge base.

For instance, at that time he did not know how to read a map. In particular, he did not know that when you look at a map, up is north, down is south, right is east, and left is west. I assumed everyone knew that, but somehow Kevin had missed learning that vital piece of information. He'd also missed a number of simple grammatical rules, lessons that I was teaching my second-grade class at the time—for example, the difference between *to* and *too*.

In sharing this, I don't intend to be critical or belittle him. I love my husband and respect his intelligence. But I was genuinely shocked to learn that a bright man in his early twenties with a college degree had these gaps in his learning. Over the next couple of years, I taught him a few grammatical rules and other small lessons he had missed growing up.

A MASSIVE LESSON MISSED

It is good to know that north on a map is upward. It is helpful to know that when using the word "too," you should be able to replace it with "also" or "excessively." But missing these things is not a spiritual tragedy or a life-altering reality. When I was in my early twenties, I discovered a lesson I had missed that was far more important than any of the things Kevin had overlooked.

I was raised by devoted, loving, and sincere Christian parents. Their faith, then and now, is an example to me. I went to a Bible-preaching church Sunday mornings and Sunday evenings and was often the last person to leave because I loved Jesus and the people of God. I attended Sunday school with teachers who delighted to see children learn about Jesus and the Bible. I even attended midweek catechism classes and learned from them. All of this, and yet I still missed an important truth.

I made a commitment to Jesus at five years old. I believed the Bible was true and the very Word of God. I read the Scriptures faithfully and did daily devotions. I attended Calvin University, a top academic school that took the Christian faith very seriously. I was immersed in a vibrant faith community and an extended family that loved Jesus. With all of this, and a flood of great biblical teaching filling my mind and heart, I have to humbly admit I missed one of the most important lessons in the Bible. Sadly, I did not realize I had missed this truth until my early twenties.

A LIFE-CHANGING REVELATION

Early in our ministry I attended a leadership conference with my husband. We were serving a church in Glendora, California, and part of our ministry was seeking out ongoing education and training to help us grow. On the second day of the event, we learned that one of the main speakers had to pull out of the event and would not be speaking. In his place, a man named Brennan Manning would be filling in for him. We had never heard of Brennan, but God was about to use this man to teach me a truth that had eluded me for two decades.

Brennan was a passionate, quirky, wiry man who spoke from the depth of his heart in a way I had seldom heard. His message was about the relentless grace of God. He was committed to helping all of us understand that God is a loving *Abba* who cares more about us than we could imagine or dream.

In his message, he told a simple story that unlocked my heart and allowed me to receive a gift I had not yet fully understood or embraced. Brennan related an account of a priest named Edward Farrell from Detroit, Michigan, who went to Ireland to celebrate the eightieth birthday of his uncle Seamus. Early on the morning of that great day, Edward and his uncle went for a long walk along the shores of Lake Killarney. As the sun crept up and warmed the earth, his uncle stood still and gazed into the morning light for almost twenty minutes, saying nothing.

Then, unexpectedly, Uncle Seamus began to skip along the shore of Lake Killarney, his face radiant with a smile from ear to ear. When Edward Farrell caught up with his uncle, he said, "Uncle Seamus, you look very happy. Do you want to tell me why?"

"Yes, lad," Uncle Seamus said, his face beaming even brighter and tears streaming down his cheeks. "You see, me Abba is very fond of me."[5]

As I sat listening, tears began to roll down my face. They were tears of wonder, sorrow, and joy mingled together. I realized that I had missed this. I could tell you that God loved me, I could quote Bible verses to support this fact, and I actually believed it! But I did not know—had not personally experienced—the truth that God was fond of me, that he liked me. I had not skipped in sheer joy because of an awareness that the God of the universe delighted in me. I had never stood in awestruck wonder at the reality that I am a beloved and cherished daughter of God.

In that moment my tears were partly for what I had missed, but more than that, they were for the gift of what I had just found. This was a truth that must have been taught to me many times, but it had never sunk in. My husband had missed lessons on how to use *to* or *too*. But I had missed the heart of the gospel that I received as a five-year-old child. I had not experienced being God's beloved.

From that day on, everything began to change. Once my heart was captured by this truth, my prayer life changed in beautiful and glorious ways.

GOD LOVES US AND HE LIKES US

The apostle Paul went through his own process of discovering the love and delight of God. Though he had been a hater of the church and a persecutor of Christians, Paul received God's amazing grace and his entire life was transformed. When our hearts open to receive the truth of God's delight over us, we are compelled to communicate with this God. Listen to the passion of Paul's prayer: "For this reason I kneel before the Father, from whom every family in heaven and on earth derives its name. I pray that out of his glorious riches he may strengthen you with power through his Spirit in your inner being, so that Christ may dwell in your hearts through faith. And I pray that you, being rooted and established in love, may have power, together with all the Lord's holy people, to grasp how wide and long and high and deep is the love of Christ, and to know this love that surpasses knowledge—that you may be filled to the measure of all the fullness of God" (Eph. 3:14–19).

Paul fell on his knees in praise for God's fatherly love. He lifted up supplication for the people of God. His desire was that followers of Jesus would grasp the greatness of God's love. The language he used is striking. How wide, long, high, and deep is this love of God. It is a love beyond measure. It surpasses knowledge. It is as if Paul was saying, "May you comprehend the massive nature of God's love for you, a love that can never be fully understood."

When I realized that God not only loves me but also likes me, my understanding of God grew. So did my awareness of who I am. I am a loved and cherished child of the Ruler of the universe. God is my *Abba*. This reality continues to transform my prayer life in four distinct ways:

1. *I pray knowing that God is radically approachable.* When I realized that God likes me, I began to believe that he likes being with me. I can enter his presence with confidence

that his arms are wide open. I remember that while Jesus was hanging on the cross, bearing my sins and paying the price for my rebellion, the curtain in the temple was torn in two from top to bottom (Matt. 27:51). It was as if the very hands of God gripped the curtain and ripped it in half. This physical divider was the visual reminder that only the high priest could enter the most holy place, and then only once a year, to offer a blood sacrifice. This curtain was a symbol of separation. When Jesus offered salvation and grace as he died on the cross, the curtain was torn and the approach to the very presence of God was opened for all of his children.

2. *I pray with growing hunger for an intimate relationship with him.* When I am confident that God loves me and likes me, I seek a closer friendship with my Creator. I am not drawn to people who don't like me. I am drawn to those who care about me. As I understand that the Father is fond of me, I hunger for a deeper relationship with him.

3. *I pray feeling free to be who I am*, even in my brokenness. I don't have to pretend or put on a show for someone who loves me and likes me. I am free to be myself. What I have learned over the years is that this freedom to be who I am releases me to become who God would have me be.

4. *I pray and my fears evaporate.* Life is full of fear—fear of rejection, judgment, abandonment, and countless other things. When I live with a clear vision of how God sees me, fear runs for the back door and heads out of town. I am not talking about awe for God's glory or even a holy fear of the almighty God of the universe. I am talking about unreasonable fears that drive me away from God. I am talking about ungodly fears instilled by the enemy. When I

embrace the perfect love of God, fear disappears like morning mist as the sun rises. The Bible teaches that "there is no fear in love. But perfect love drives out fear, because fear has to do with punishment. The one who fears is not made perfect in love" (1 John 4:18).

The love of God for you and me is so great that the only picture that comes close to reflecting God's heart is his beloved Son hanging on a cruel cross, bearing our sin and shame and offering us his righteousness (2 Cor. 5:21). No matter how much we think we understand this gift and comprehend God's love, there is still more to learn. There is more to be received. There is always more!

A RIGHT VIEW OF GOD

Our view of God affects every aspect of our lives and faith. The great pastor and theologian A. W. Tozer penned these words: "What comes into our mind when we think about God is the most important thing about us. . . . Were we able to extract from any man a complete answer to the question, 'What comes into your mind when you think about God?' we might predict with certainty the spiritual future of that man."[6]

If we view God as disinterested, we will not draw near him. If we view God as a kind but weak old man in the sky, we will not trust him to deliver in times of need. If we believe God is an angry judge looking for a reason to throw the book at us, we will run away and hide from him. But when we know that God loves us and is fond of us, we run to his arms with trust and confidence that he wants the best for us. This leads to prayer at all times and in all places.

GOD'S LOVE FOR THE WORLD

In the gospel of John, right after Jesus' encounter with Nicodemus, we read these words: "For God so loved the world that he gave his one and only Son, that whoever believes in him shall not perish but have eternal life. For God did not send his Son into the world to condemn the world, but to save the world through him. Whoever believes in him is not condemned, but whoever does not believe stands condemned already because they have not believed in the name of God's one and only Son" (John 3:16–18).

God's love extends beyond those who are already in the church and part of his family. God's love is big enough for the whole world.

Kevin and I have spent almost four decades serving the local church. We have also spent these years training and helping other churches, denominational leaders, and international leaders as they seek to be outwardly focused and develop a culture of evangelistic faithfulness. We use the term "Organic Outreach" (see organic outreach.org) to describe the practice of sharing God's love and good news naturally. We believe that God's heart for the world should move our hearts to action and to passionate and persistent organic prayers for those who are still far from Jesus.

HENRY'S STORY

Deb was the last of five children born to Henry and Betty. She grew up in a caring family that had no Christian faith. Her father, Henry, was a farmer and loved to share his produce with friends and neighbors. Deb loved her family and felt very loved by her parents.

When Deb met Bruce, they fell in love, got married, and started their own family. Bruce was a Christian, and Deb soon discovered the love and grace of Jesus. She received the Savior, joined a local church, and began growing in her newfound faith. When she told her father she had become a Christian, she thought he would be happy for her. Instead, he said, "You can do what you want, but I think you are making a mistake."

These words broke her heart and motivated her to begin praying for her father. Months and years passed and Henry showed no sign of opening his heart to God's love and grace. Deb would find herself wondering, "Why am I trying so hard and praying so much? It does not seem to be making a difference." Instead of giving up, she committed to keep praying and invited others to pray for her dad also. About two decades into her prayer journey, as Deb shared her heart for her dad, I made a commitment to pray for my dear friend's father. Deb also opened the door for Kevin to visit her dad and build a friendship.

Over the next decade Kevin developed a relationship with Henry. I made a commitment to Deb that I would pray for her dad every time I drove past his house, which was about a dozen times every week. I told Deb that I would do my best to let his home remind me to pray for him. Through the years Henry showed no signs of softening his heart, but we kept praying and loving him. We all knew that Jesus loved Henry, and we longed to see him embrace the amazing grace of the Savior.

When Henry was in his late eighties, they found out he had bone cancer. It was advanced and the doctors were clear that Henry did not have much more time on this earth. Deb kept praying and cried out to the Lord to send medical professionals who loved Jesus and who would add their voices to the others who were sharing the gospel with him. In the coming days many prayed, and one of the medical helpers shared the story of Jesus with Henry, but all outward appearances made it clear that he was not interested.

After a long day at the hospital, with a report from the doctor that Henry's condition was growing worse and he did not have much more time, Deb took her mom home to sleep and stayed with her for the night. All who knew Deb increased their prayers, along with Deb. She cried out to God late into the night, lifting up honest prayers and shedding many tears.

About four in the morning, Deb woke up to the sound of bells ringing. She walked around the living room, trying to figure out where this beautiful music was coming from and concluded it must be from the clock in the living room. When Deb's mom woke up, Deb asked her about the clock and the beautiful music it played, but her mom assured her the clock was broken and had not been working for years.

A short time later they headed to the hospital to visit Henry. When Deb walked into the room, she was shocked when she saw tears streaming down her father's face. He had an uncommon radiance to his countenance, and he said, "Debbie, come over here. I have to tell you something. I know you will understand." Deb came close and looked into his face. Henry said, "You don't have to worry anymore. I met Jesus. He came to me today." Deb was overjoyed and breathless. Later, as she reflected on the bells and music she had heard that morning, she concluded that God, in his grace and mercy, had allowed her to know the moment that her earthly father met Jesus. In the last days of his life, Henry encountered the Savior and discovered that the Father was fond of him. Henry lived for a little more than a week after that precious morning and then went home to his loving heavenly Father.

I still remember the first time I drove by Henry's house after he passed away. I reflexively wanted to pray, since I had done it so many times over the previous years. Instead of my regular prayer for Henry, I simply praised the Father for his love and grace.

I also thanked God for the privilege of sharing in Henry's journey through praying as I drove by his house. As best I can tell, I prayed for Henry's heart to soften and receive the Father's love through Jesus more than a dozen times each week for nine years. His daughter Deb had prayed far more than that—she had prayed for her father for more than thirty years. When you add the prayers of all Deb's family and friends, the number is staggering. As I drove on, I thought how much God must love Henry to move so many people to pray for him all those years, including me, a person who had never met him face to face. It was truly God's love for Henry that moved me to pray all those years. This is the heart of the Father. Our prayers were a small reflection of the greatness of God's love.

DRIVE-BY PRAYERS

In the months that followed, Deb talked to me about how she had begun praying as she drove by other people's homes. She shared how my example of praying for her father with my eyes wide open had inspired her to do what she now calls "drive-by prayers."

Imagine what could happen if every Christian developed a habit of doing drive-by prayers. Christians would pray more for people they know—and, as in my case with Henry, some they don't even know—as they drive by different reminder points.

Maybe God's Spirit would stir you to start praying for local churches. Whenever you drive or pass by a church, you would pray for God's blessings, for a great work of the Holy Spirit among that fellowship of believers, and for that local church to love and serve their community by sharing the good news of Jesus in natural ways. What might God do through those prayers?

Police and firefighters would be lifted up and prayers for

protection and wisdom would be lavished on them as the Holy Spirit reminded believers to pray as they drive by their local police station or firehouse. Civic leaders would be covered in prayer as believers drive by and ask God to bless those in places of community leadership and influence. You might be moved to lift up prayers for schools, teachers, administrators, and students each time you drive by a place of education. As Christians drive and pray with their eyes open, power would be unleashed and lives would be changed.

When we realize, in the core of our being, that the Father is fond of us, we recognize that he is also fond of the people we encounter each day. We take delight in knowing we are loved and liked. And we are moved to love, serve, and pray for the people God brings across our path each day.

I pray that if I live to be eighty years old, someone will look at me and ask, "Why do you look so happy?" If they do, I will say, "You see, me Abba is very fond of me. My Father is so very fond of me." But more than this, I hope I can tell people this truth every day of my life. It is my prayer that you also will know that the Father is fond of you, which seems to be a good reason to skip and smile.

YOUR PRAYER JOURNEY

Take a walk with the God who loves you. Spend time on your walk asking God to help you understand how fond he is of you. If you have a sense that he loves you and likes you, feel free to skip! If someone asks you why you are skipping, you know what to tell them: "The Father is fond of me!" When you know the Father is fond of you, you discover that he is fond of others.

Identify one person you know who lives near you and who is not yet a follower of Jesus. Commit to pray for this person each time you go by his or her home. Ask for God to open this person's heart and eyes to his grace. Pray for courage and opportunities to share God's love and message of grace with this person.

Chapter Ten

HONEST TO GOD

*It is of great importance, when we begin
to practice prayer, not to let ourselves be
frightened by our own thoughts.*
—Teresa of Ávila

CAN WE BE TOTALLY HONEST with God in prayer? Should we be? I believe the answer to both of these questions is a bold "Yes!" For many years I was confused about this topic. I can't identify exactly where it came from, but I had a sense that it might be disrespectful or dishonoring to tell God everything that was on my heart. Being well aware of my own sinfulness and brokenness caused me to hold back and not pray with unrestrained transparency.

It was my love for the book of Psalms that brought me to a place of breakthrough. As I immersed myself in these biblical prayers, the Holy Spirit gave me insight, clarity, and fresh conviction that honest prayers not only are allowed but please God. Throughout the Psalms, I heard other passionate followers of God bring their pain, fear, questions, anger, and struggles into the presence of the Lord of glory. These prayers struck me as raw, vulnerable, shocking at times, and encouraging.

As I began praying the psalms and letting these ancient songs pray for me, honesty began to feel natural. Rather than irreverent, my truthful prayers felt God-honoring. Instead of creating a sense of guilt, they freed me to pour out my heart and discover new depths of grace.

OUT OF THE DEPTHS

On my journey toward honest prayer, I was introduced to a book simply titled *Out of the Depths*. In this insightful book, Bernhard W. Anderson introduces the psalms of lament and the form of the laments. These are a category of psalms that are cries of pain, loss, fear, brokenness, and despair. For years I had been praying these psalms and letting them pray for me, but I was unaware that there was a specific kind of prayer titled "lament." I did not know that many others had walked this same road of discovery and had grown to love these prayers and hold on to them in their hard times.

Dietrich Bonhoeffer, the martyred Christian pastor who resisted the Nazi regime, loved the psalms. He regarded the book of Psalms as his favorite book in the Bible. These prayers would have been on his heart and lips as he suffered in the Flossenbürg concentration camp and as he was executed because of his faith and dissent. His last publication before his execution was *The Prayer Book of the Bible: An Introduction to the Psalms* (1940). In this writing he developed the idea that just as Jesus Christ has taught us to pray the words of the Lord's Prayer, the book of Psalms, "the prayer book of the Bible," guides and instructs us in greater fullness the words that God wants us to speak to him in the name of Jesus Christ.[7] I became aware that I was part of a community of Christians who turned to the psalms as both an instructor and a friend in the furnace of life.

As I learned from Anderson, Bonhoeffer, and others, a fresh picture formed in my mind. God not only welcomes prayers of lament but also gives them to us to affirm that there will be times when prayers like this will spill from our hearts and lips.

Just before the first verse of Psalm 102, there is a simple and telling superscription: "A prayer of an afflicted person who has grown weak and pours out a lament before the Lord." Wow, what an introduction! What follows are raw, honest, tear-streaked words:

> Hear my prayer, Lord;
>> let my cry for help come to you.
> Do not hide your face from me
>> when I am in distress.
> Turn your ear to me;
>> when I call, answer me quickly.
>
> For my days vanish like smoke;
>> my bones burn like glowing embers.
> My heart is blighted and withered like grass;
>> I forget to eat my food.
> In my distress I groan aloud
>> and am reduced to skin and bones.
> I am like a desert owl,
>> like an owl among the ruins.
> I lie awake; I have become
>> like a bird alone on a roof.
> All day long my enemies taunt me;

those who rail against me use my name as a curse.
For I eat ashes as my food
and mingle my drink with tears.

—verses 1–9

The lesson I am still learning is that, at its core, prayer is an honest conversation with the God who is absolute truth. When our prayers lack honesty, they lack power. Praying with an open heart means recognizing that God already sees everything, even what we wish was hidden. This frees us to express ourselves with intentional transparency because we know that God is sovereign and omniscient. He knows everything about us and still loves us.

A STRUCTURE AND A FLOW

As I learned more about the psalms of lament, I found that there are many groups or types of psalms in the Bible. Some of these are thanksgiving psalms, wisdom psalms, royal psalms (about the king), messianic psalms (pointing to the Messiah, Jesus), psalms of ascent (to be sung while going on pilgrimage to Jerusalem), and psalms of lament. Of all the categories of psalms, the laments, perhaps surprisingly, are the largest group; more than one-third of all the psalms are laments. Not only are these the most common, but there is a consistent structure that most laments follow. As I learned the flow of prayer within the laments, it shaped my honest prayers in times of sorrow, loss, and struggle. Not every lament psalm follows this pattern exactly, but the general flow goes something like this:

1. Address to God: calling out to God using one of his names or attributes

2. Honest and heartfelt complaint: whatever you are facing—sickness, fear of enemies, awareness of sin, physical pain, relational brokenness, heartache—poured out with shocking truthfulness

3. Confession of trust in God: a bold declaration that God is still powerful and present no matter what we face

4. Petition for needs: an honest cry for help in the midst of the storm and a plea for strength to overcome

5. Words of assurance: an expression of trust that this prayer is being heard by God Almighty

6. Vow of praise: a confident declaration of continued praise and worship[8]

Even with a quick and simple review of these six movements, we can see the beauty of how God is teaching us to pray from the heart. The flow matches a heart that loves and trusts God but is also being ravaged by the storms of life.

A prayer of lament begins as a man or woman cries out to God. Because there is a relationship, there is some form of direct address. "Hear my prayer, Lord" (Ps. 102:1) and "My God, my God" (Ps. 22:1) are examples of this natural address. Prayer is speaking to God, so calling out one of his names is appropriate and part of the structure of a lament.

Next, and often the largest part of the prayer, is an honest complaint. Expressions of sorrow, pain, fear, frustration, and even anger are poured out with candid and passionate words. As we saw in Psalm 102, this can range from physical pain, to loneliness, to fear of enemies, to sadness. All of these are expressed in the same psalm in the portion called the complaint.

In the midst of this candid expression of pain and sorrow, there is almost always a point when the person praying pauses and declares trust and confidence in God. Though in pain and feeling broken, the supplicant still lives with an abiding certainty that God is God, he is on the throne, and he can be trusted . . . no matter what. In Psalm 102, right after crying out, "My days are like the evening shadow; I wither away like grass," the psalmist declares, "But you, LORD, sit enthroned forever; your renown endures through all generations" (vv. 11–12). As we learn to be honest to God in prayer, it is critical that we declare our trust and confidence, even as we pour out our struggles and pain.

Since we are praying to the God who is able to do all things, it is natural, even when honestly expressing struggle, to ask him for help. This is why psalms of lament almost always move into a time of humble and honest petition. If the person praying has lamented the attacks of an enemy, there is often a prayer for victory over that foe. If it is sickness or physical torment, a prayer for healing follows. If the complaint is the battle with sin, power for repentance and turning around is sought. Whatever the lament might be, a prayer for the situation to change should flow naturally from our hearts and lips.

Finally, the person praying declares something like, "I will declare your name to my people; in the assembly I will praise you" (Ps. 22:22). Before we finish a prayer of lament, our trust and confidence in God's goodness and worthiness compel us to express our assurance that our prayers are being heard and that we will continue to praise him.

These six elements in a lament prayer are often found in this exact order: address, complaint, trust, petition, assurance, and praise. Sometimes an element can be missing. At other times the order can be slightly different. There are even times a prayer in the psalms might cycle back to complaint, praise, or an expression of need more than once. The point is not that an exact order needs to be followed. What we realize is that when our hearts enter God's presence, our expressions of honest pain, declarations of continued trust, cries for help, and commitment to praise God, even in the greatest storms of life, flow from the depths of our souls to the God who welcomes these rugged and raw expressions of honest prayer. When we pray this way, we join the ancients in God-honoring lament and profoundly transparent prayer.

CONFUSION, COMPLAINT, AND CLARITY

In Psalm 73 we have a beautiful opportunity to peek into the heart and journey of a passionate person of prayer. Through this prayer of Asaph, we discover that honesty in prayer leads to clarity of thought and a confident heart. Too often we seek to live our days guided by our own wisdom and understanding. In the third chapter of Proverbs we are warned not to trust in our own understanding: "Trust in the LORD with all your heart and lean not on your own understanding; in all your ways submit to him, and he will make your paths straight" (vv. 5–6). Honest prayer can actually crystallize our thinking and teach us to trust God at deeper levels.

The prayer in Psalm 73 begins with a declaration of belief: "Surely God is good to Israel, to those who are pure in heart" (v. 1). This is a confident proclamation. On the heels of this comes an emotional expression of what the psalmist is feeling: "But as for me, my feet had almost slipped; I had nearly lost my foothold. For I envied the arrogant when I saw the prosperity of the wicked" (vv. 2–3). He goes on to reflect on the wicked and arrogant and observes that they seem to prosper and get away with their evil practices (vv. 4–12). There is a sense of honest despair and a heavy heart about the injustice of people who walk far from God, rebel against the Lord, and still seem to come up smelling like roses.

The psalmist is confused and complaining. The world does not make sense. His observations and insight can't sort things out. His frustration culminates in the expression, "When I tried to understand all this, it troubled me deeply" (v. 16). With honest words and a transparent heart, he tells God that the world does not make sense.

The turning point of this psalmist's spiritual journey comes when he draws near to God, as seen in verse 17: "Till I entered the sanctuary of God; then I understood their final destiny." Truth breaks through. His eyes are opened to the true fate of the wicked (vv. 18–20). Assurance floods in, hope is reborn, clarity is found in honest prayer. With his final words the writer declares, "But as for me, it is good to be near God. I have made the Sovereign LORD my refuge; I will tell of all your deeds" (v. 28). You can feel the peace of God calming the psalmist's heart as his confidence is bolstered.

When we face confusion and turmoil over the injustice of the world and the growth of evil around us, the answer is not to try to figure everything out in our own understanding. We should bring our frustrations and pain to God with bold confession of our inability to make sense of things. As we do this with humble honesty, God brings the clarity we can't attain on our own. As we draw near God in prayer, he gently pulls back the veil that covers our eyes and hearts and shows us his glory, his power, his presence, and his plan.

GOD INVITES US TO COME WITH HONEST PRAYERS

Over and over God extends an invitation to draw near him as we are, with authentic prayers, even when we are hurting and confused. Read these passages slowly and reflectively. Hear the invitation God extends for you to come and speak your heart with boldness:

"Because he loves me," says the LORD, "I will rescue him;
    I will protect him, for he acknowledges my name.
He will call on me, and I will answer him;
    I will be with him in trouble,
    I will deliver him and honor him.
With long life I will satisfy him
    and show him my salvation."

—Psalm 91:14-16

I love the LORD, for he heard my voice;
    he heard my cry for mercy.
Because he turned his ear to me,
    I will call on him as long as I live.
The cords of death entangled me,
    the anguish of the grave came over me;
    I was overcome by distress and sorrow.
Then I called on the name of the LORD:
    "LORD, save me!"

—Psalm 116:1-4

The LORD is near to all who call on him,
    to all who call on him in truth.
He fulfills the desires of those who fear him;
    he hears their cry and saves them.

—Psalm 145:18-19

Come, all you who are thirsty,
    come to the waters;
and you who have no money,
    come, buy and eat!
Come, buy wine and milk

without money and without cost. . . .
Give ear and come to me;
   listen, that you may live.
I will make an everlasting covenant with you,
   my faithful love promised to David.

—Isaiah 55:1, 3

Call to me and I will answer you and tell you great and unsearchable things you do not know.

—Jeremiah 33:3

But as for me, I watch in hope for the LORD,
   I wait for God my Savior;
   my God will hear me.

—Micah 7:7

While some may think God does not tolerate our prayers from the depths of our sorrow, confusion, and pain, he actually invites them. He waits for them. He hears these prayers because he loves us.

JESUS MODELED HONEST PRAYERS OF LAMENT

When Jesus was hanging on the cross bearing our sins and taking our shame, he prayed. In his hour of need and sorrow, Jesus quoted a lament psalm and made it his own. Our Savior pierced the sky as he cried out, "My God, my God, why have you forsaken me?" (Ps. 22:1). Every Jewish person on the hill of Golgotha would have recognized these words inspired through King David a thousand years earlier. Jesus went to the prayer book of God's people and let the words become his own.

If you have any worry about being honest with God and letting the psalms of lament become part of your prayer life, worry no longer. Jesus shows us the way forward on our spiritual journey, and the Savior gave us an example of honest prayer as he offered his own life and blood to open the way for us to be saved and come home to the Father.

GOD CAN HANDLE YOUR HONESTY

Maybe you were raised to believe it is irreverent, undignified, or even ungodly to be entirely honest with God in prayer. In his book *You'll Get through This*, Max Lucado gives this advice for Christians who are walking through a time of great pain, struggle, and confusion: "Pray your pain out. Pound the table. March up and down the lawn. It's time for tenacious, honest prayers. Angry at God? Disappointed with his strategy? Ticked off at his choices? Let him know it."[9] I love this challenge, and I have been learning to live it out. I am discovering that the more honest I am, the more vibrant my prayer life becomes. The more transparent I become, the more intimate I feel with my God.

Stop and think about what we are saying when we lock up our frustration and swallow our sorrow. We are acting as though God can't handle our honest expressions of pain and anger. We are pretending that God does not know. But God searches our hearts and nothing is hidden from his eyes. God knows everything about us, even what we try to hide.

In Psalm 139, David reflects on what God knows about us. God searches us and sees everything. He knows our actions, thoughts, and words. The Maker of the universe even knows the words we choose not to say: "Before a word is on my tongue you, LORD, know it completely" (v. 4). There is no place in all creation where God is not present. Even in our mother's wombs, God was there, intimately making us and caring for us. God knows every day of our lives, before even one transpires. Since God knows everything, let's not hold back. It is time to start praying with new levels of honesty and frankness.

POURING OUT, NOT POURING IN!

One of my favorite women in the Bible is Hannah. We meet this great woman of faith and hear her story in the first two chapters of 1 Samuel. She has suffered with barrenness for at least a decade. In a culture where having children was seen as a heavenly blessing, Hannah felt dejected and forgotten by God. In the depths of sorrow she came into the house of God in Shiloh. Out of a place of deep trouble and heartache, she prayed and cried out to God. Her suffering was so profound that she had no words, but she moved her lips as she poured out her heart to her Maker.

What happened next only compounded her sorrow. The priest, Eli, accused her of being drunk. Her heart was so broken and her behavior so severe that the elderly priest assumed she was under the influence: "How long are you going to stay drunk? Put away your wine" (1:14). Hannah's response is an example for all of us: "'Not so, my lord,' Hannah replied, 'I am a woman who is deeply troubled. I have not been drinking wine or beer; I was pouring out my soul to the LORD. Do not take your servant for a wicked woman; I have been praying here out of my great anguish and grief'" (1:15–16). She corrects the great Eli and explains that she is pouring out, not pouring in. In times of pain, loss, and suffering, these seem to be the two common and opposite responses.

We can seek to medicate our hurt, confusion, and shattered hearts by pouring in drink, drugs, food, shopping, work, or other things intended to numb our pain. Or we can pour out our hearts with honest prayer. We can come before God and tell him exactly what we are feeling. We can admit our fear, uncover our shame, express our anger, and open our hearts to the God who already knows everything about us and has proven his unending love through the ultimate sacrifice, his own life.

If being honest to God has not been a part of your prayer life or is an area that needs to be developed, it is my prayer that you will let the Scriptures speak for you and direct you as you continue on this journey of learning how to pray with your heart wide open to God.

YOUR PRAYER JOURNEY

Use the simple structure of a lament psalm and pray your own lament to God. Be as honest as you can and be sure to declare your trust as well as your pain and struggles. Ask God to show you what you tend to pour into yourself when you should be pouring out your sorrow and heartache to him. Pray for power to stop pouring in when you should be pouring out.

Chapter Eleven

WARFARE PRAYERS

God's child can conquer everything by prayer. Is it any
wonder that Satan does his utmost to snatch that weapon
from the Christian or to hinder him in the use of it?
—Andrew Murray

MY FIRSTBORN SON, Zach, was heading off to full days of
school for the first time. He would get on a bus and head out, away
from my care, away from my sight, away from my protection and
motherly love, but not away from my prayers. I needed to go deeper
in prayer and trust God with greater intensity as I released my son
for the better part of a day.

I was drawn to read John 17, Jesus' High Priestly Prayer.
I wanted to learn from the Master and hungered to know how to
pray for those I love the most, and this portion of the Bible is where
Jesus prays for his beloved disciples. I had read John 17 many times
through my years of following Jesus, but this time the context and
unique setting of my life presented a fresh opening that the wind
of God's Spirit could blow through.

Shortly after Jesus lifted up this prayer, he would die on the cross. He would bear our sins and conquer death. He would take his last breath, be placed in a tomb for three days, and be raised in power. After a time of teaching and ministry, he would ascend to the Father. His disciples, his followers and spiritual children, would not have him with them day in and day out. Yes, Jesus would send the Holy Spirit to be with and in them. But he would not be physically present to walk with them. With this reality in mind, Jesus prayed for them.

When I faced the reality that my children would be out of the shadow of my motherly wings, I learned to pray in new ways. As I read this powerful prayer of the Savior, it struck me that this is a spiritual warfare prayer. I had never read it this way before. Several verses gripped my heart, opened my eyes, and transformed my prayer life: "I will remain in the world no longer, but they are still in the world, and I am coming to you. Holy Father, protect them by the power of your name, the name you gave me, so that they may be one as we are one. While I was with them, I protected them and kept them safe by that name you gave me. . . . My prayer is not that you take them out of the world but that you protect them from the evil one. They are not of the world, even as I am not of it" (John 17:11–12, 15–16).

Jesus cried out for his spiritual children. He would not be with them, but the power of the Father is always enough to protect and save. Jesus knew they would be in the world, so he prayed for protection from the Evil One. This truth began to shape practices of prayer that still remain with me years later.

PROTECTION PRAYERS

Zach was in first grade. Josh and Nate were preschoolers. As they moved out of my circle of protection, I prayed more. And as they grew older, I would go even deeper in prayer for them. When all three were off to school, sporting events, and overnight times with friends, I would pray, "Holy God, in the power of the name of Jesus, protect my boys. They do not belong to this world. They are yours. I do not pray that you remove them from this world; it is my prayer that your light shines through them in the darkness of the world they live in. I do pray that you protect them from the Evil One, the prince of this world" (see John 12:31). These protection prayers took on new dimensions and intensity when they started driving, when they went off to college, and, even now, as they have become adults and are married.

As my sons were growing up, I had a sense that my nurturing-mother role changed with each new season. I had to work on lessening those mothering tendencies and loosening my grip. But there was one area I found my attention and intention could increase as they grew older: my prayer life for them. This piece of our relationship didn't need to decrease but instead could grow with the passing years.

The prayer of Jesus for his disciples has profoundly shaped my prayers. There is rarely a day that Kevin and I do not pray together for each of our boys and now their wives and our grandchildren as well. We pray like Jesus did, "Lord, we do not pray for you to take them from the world; we believe you have called them to shine their light while in this world. Protect them from the enemy in the power of your glorious name."

As I look back, I realize my practice of praying for them as young children revealed something about my faith. I had a sense that when they were near me, I did not have to pray as intensely and passionately. I believed I could protect them and meet their needs when they were physically near. Now I know that only God's grace is enough to keep my sons, my husband, my extended family and friends, and any person safe. Only God's power is sufficient.

Now I begin each day in prayer. As I roll out of bed and onto my knees, among other things I ask for God's presence and power to protect me, my family, and others as well. I believe one of the greatest signs of true love is praying for people like this, praying for them as Jesus prayed for his disciples in his longest prayer recorded in the Bible.

HERE IS THE BAD NEWS

The human family can be broken into two groups of people when it comes to personal preferences of hearing good and bad news. There are those who want to hear the bad news first—and those who want to hear the good news first. In this enduring debate, I am firmly in the former group. Give me the bad news and make it quick. I just want to get it over with.

So, for those of you like me, here is the bad news: *You have an enemy!*

This enemy has many names: Satan, the devil, thief, and tempter, just to name a few. Peter tells us that our enemy "prowls around like a roaring lion looking for someone to devour" (1 Peter 5:8). He is a spiritual being of great power and intelligence, created by God, who has rebelled against God and is now at war with God's people. Your enemy is real and he wants to destroy your life. He is deceitful, active, perpetually looking for a point of attack. He does not simply want to nibble on the edges of your life, he wants to swallow you whole and devour you.

Jesus tells us that the enemy of your soul is a "thief [who] comes only to steal and kill and destroy" (John 10:10). Satan wants to rob you of all that is good and beautiful. He is a killer from the beginning. He delights to destroy all the good things God has created. Don't let anyone give you the false impression that the devil has some people he likes and favors. The enemy only hates, kills, destroys, and deceives. There is no good in him.

Did you realize there is a being in this universe who is alive and actively seeking to "steal and kill and destroy"? Some people say Satan is alive and well. I say he is alive, but he is not well! He is dead set against you being spiritually alive and thriving in the power of God. You bear the image of the almighty Ruler of the universe. You carry the message of the gospel in your heart and on your lips. Because of this, the enemy hates you. He can do nothing to destroy your position and identity in Christ. But he will relentlessly seek to distract, deceive, and tempt you.

This is why we must pray. We make a tenacious choice to be people of prayer at all times, in all places, making prayer a natural part of our lives—organic prayers. There is a real enemy, but there is also a victorious weapon called prayer. Organic prayers unleash the power of heaven.

HERE IS THE GOOD NEWS

When Jesus was getting ready to leave this world, he prayed for the protection of his children against the enemy. He sent the Holy Spirit to be in us and with us (John 14:15–21). God's Word assures us that "the one who is in you is greater than the one who is in the world" (1 John 4:4). We have power to resist temptation, fight the enemy, and walk in victory. Jesus came to give us life, and life to the fullest (John 10:10).

Jesus himself prayed for his followers to be protected from the enemy. This should assure us that our enemy is real but the victory has already been won. Jesus conquered sin and the devil. Though

God has won, we still need to stand strong and resist the enemy's enticements, reject his lies, and walk in the power of Jesus. Prayer becomes one of the weapons for the battle.

A POWERFUL EXAMPLE AND EXHORTATION

Patrice is a friend and spiritual mentor. She has traveled down the road of faith a few decades farther than I. Patrice sang with Bob Hope on the USO tours during the Korean War and has held the hand of Jesus as three husbands have passed away. She is now in her nineties and is a person of perpetual joy, constant grace, and tenacious faith-filled prayer.

In one of our conversations Patrice encouraged me to begin each day reading Ephesians 6:10–18 just as she has done for many years. I took her advice and for the past several years I have started my day on my knees praying, and then opening my Bible and reading these challenging words:

Finally, be strong in the Lord and in his mighty power. Put on the full armor of God, so that you can take your stand against the devil's schemes. For our struggle is not against flesh and blood, but against the rulers, against the authorities, against the powers of this dark world and against the spiritual forces of evil in the heavenly realms. Therefore put on the full armor of God, so that when the day of evil comes, you may be able to stand your ground, and after you have done everything, to stand. Stand firm then, with the belt of truth buckled around your waist, with the breastplate of righteousness in place, and with your feet fitted with the readiness that comes from the gospel of peace. In addition to all this, take up the shield of faith, with which you can extinguish all the flaming arrows of the evil one. Take the helmet of salvation and the sword of the Spirit, which is the word of God.

And pray in the Spirit on all occasions with all kinds of prayers and requests. With this in mind, be alert and always keep on praying for all the Lord's people.

I have not tired of this spiritual discipline. Each morning the Holy Spirit of God reminds me that walking into our world is an invitation to battle. These words of Scripture make me mindful of the enemy, the armor I must put on, and the absolute promise that God will help me stand, no matter what I face. I do not have to succumb to defeat. I can walk in victory! And so can you!

As I have read, studied, and meditated on these words from Ephesians 6, a singular reality has gripped my soul and pierced my life: *the battle is real and the enemy is close at hand.* I am not paranoid, but I am prepared for the spiritual battle that awaits me as I move into every single day.

It is impossible to read the words of Jesus and examine his life and miss the fact that our Lord fought spiritual battles. Our Savior could see behind the veil of this world and recognize the presence and power of the enemy. If we are to live like Jesus, we must learn from his example. In the fourth chapters of both Matthew and Luke, we see Jesus in fierce hand-to-hand combat with the devil. This is at the start of his public ministry. Then, near the end of his ministry, Jesus warns his followers, "Watch and pray so that you will not fall into temptation. The spirit is willing, but the flesh is weak" (Matt. 26:41). From start to finish, and everywhere in between, Jesus was engaged in the battle, and he stands as the example to his followers through all generations.

BEWARE OF THE TWO EXTREMES

As we become more like Jesus and enter the spiritual battles around us, we should be careful that we do not slip into the two extremes concerning the reality of spiritual warfare and the presence of the devil. In his classic book *The Screwtape Letters*, C. S. Lewis describes two groups of people that the devil is thrilled about.

Lewis calls our attention to the *substitious*—the skeptics. These people are not aware of the existence of a spiritual enemy. They are sure Satan is not real and that the devil exists only in the vivid imagination of children or uneducated and simple people. These confident folks are certain that the spiritual world does not exist and that no one should fear devils or demons.

Satan is thrilled with this outlook, because he can walk right in and have his way with these people. They don't stand guard or prepare for a battle, because they are sure there is no enemy. We need to beware that this kind of hubris does not mark our thinking or outlook.

Lewis also warns us about the *superstitious*. They are sure the devil and demons are behind every bush, every rock, car, and corner. Paranoia sets in as these people live with a constant fear of the enemy and a certainty that an attack is coming at all times.

Satan loves this attitude, because those who think this way can be paralyzed and made ineffective by their fear. These people are so focused on the presence of the enemy that their eyes are no longer on the risen Savior, their glorious God, and the powerful Holy Spirit. That is why praying with your eyes open to the presence and power of God is essential.

When we are aware of the enemy and prepared for the battle, we are not skeptics. We acknowledge the presence and the work of the enemy. But neither are we superstitious. Our focus is not on the enemy but on our Maker and Savior. We are not paralyzed by fear but amazed by grace and empowered by the Spirit for the battles we will face.

ARMOR AND WEAPONS FOR THE BATTLE

In Ephesians 6 we see a list of defensive armor we should put on so we can walk in victory as we face spiritual battles. We are to put on the full armor of God, and I would encourage that you do this, in prayer, whenever you feel you are headed into battle.

My suggestion is that you pray, "Lord, I put on the belt of truth, may it be tight against my waist. I put on the breastplate; let your righteousness be mine. Fit my feet with the gospel of peace and make me surefooted for the battle. I hold the shield of faith and ask that I can use it to block and put out every flaming arrow the enemy shoots at me. Cover my head and mind with the helmet of salvation."

One by one, put on the pieces of spiritual armor.

Once you have done this, you have a great defensive plan. But without offensive tactics and weapons, all you can do is protect yourself. God wants to win the victory. For this to happen, we must take up the weapons he gives for the battle. The first weapon is the sword of the Spirit, which is the Word of God (Eph. 6:17). God's Word can be used to fight back and cut down the enemy. If you wonder about this, just read the accounts of Jesus' wilderness battles with the enemy. In Matthew 4 and Luke 4, we see the Savior intensely fighting against the devil. Over and over our Lord quotes from the Word of God in the Old Testament with the declaration, "It is written!" There is no question that the Scriptures are a powerful weapon for our spiritual battles.

Prayer is also a weapon. Right after calling us to take up the sword, the apostle Paul writes: "And *pray* in the Spirit on all occasions with all kinds of *prayers* and *requests*. With this in mind, be alert and always keep on *praying* for all the Lord's people. *Pray* also for me, that whenever I speak, words may be given me so that I will fearlessly make known the mystery of the gospel, for which I am an ambassador in chains. *Pray* that I may declare it fearlessly, as I should" (Eph. 6:18–20, emphases added).

Take note of how many times the word "pray" is used in this short passage. We are called to use the power of prayer as we fight the enemy and enter spiritual battles.

Some scholars think prayer is the seventh piece of warfare equipment. Others see it as an attitude and behavior that is used with all the pieces of armor. I believe it is the latter of these two. Theologian Klyne Snodgrass explains it this way: "Whether prayer is a seventh piece of equipment is debated. Grammar suggests it is not, or else being alert, which is a parallel to praying, would have to be considered a piece of the equipment as well. But the question is irrelevant, for whether it is a piece of the equipment or the demeanor with which the equipment is worn, neither prayer nor being alert is optional for believers. By definition, to be Christ's soldier is to pray and keep alert."[10]

The heartbeat of this idea is that we pray as we put on each piece of our spiritual armor. We pray as we wear the armor through every battle. Prayer becomes not only preparation for the battle but the battle itself, as we walk and live in the power of the Holy Spirit.

Organic prayer puts us in a posture of readiness. When we pray with eyes open, ears open, hearts open, and lives open, we can pray at all times. In the battles we face with the enemy of our souls, we must be vigilant and always on our guard. This reality pierced my soul many years ago when three things happened to me at the same time.

First, I was preparing to speak at the Organic Outreach Conference, a gathering of believers who want to effectively share the good news of Jesus as a natural part of their lifestyle. Every time I speak on the topic of personal evangelism, there is an intensified spiritual battle. Second, I was reflecting on the writings of Dr. Klyne Snodgrass and his commentary on Ephesians 6. His profound insights heightened my need to be ready for spiritual battles all the time. Third and finally, I was talking and praying with Patrice, the dear woman who has discipled me and invested in my spiritual life for well over a decade. As I shared earlier in this chapter, she encouraged me to begin each day reading the spiritual armor passage found in Ephesians 6.

As these three things merged in my heart and soul, I was overwhelmed by a conviction from the Holy Spirit. I am a soldier! For the rest of my life, I need to be profoundly aware of the devil's tactics and prepared to fight back. If God is using ordinary Christians to share the extraordinary good news of Jesus, we need to stand strong, pray at all times, and follow the leading of the Holy Spirit of the Living God.

ALL THE *ALLS*

As we learn to pray with our eyes, ears, and hearts open, we will discover the power of prayer for the battle. In Ephesians 6 we are reminded that we can and should be praying at all times. Notice the word "all" and how it is used, over and over, in one simple verse: "And pray in the Spirit on *all* occasions with *all* kinds of prayers and requests. With this in mind, be alert and always keep on praying for *all* the Lord's people" (v. 18, emphases added).

There is a universal and sweeping sense to warfare prayers. We are praying on all occasions. There are not moments when we drop our guard and act as though the battle is over. Every moment provides an opportunity to see the spiritual battles around us and enter in through passionate and faith-filled prayers. We lift up all kinds of prayers with our eyes open physically or figuratively as we live for Jesus. As we give praise and thanks, we battle the enemy and exalt Jesus, the Victor. As we confess sin and ask for power to repent, we see spiritual strongholds broken and God's glory revealed. As we declare the name of Jesus and pray in his authority, the enemy flees and battles are won.

We are also called to pray for all of God's people. That is a massive undertaking. Praying for all of God's people means lifting up other believers not only in our churches, communities, and nation but also in other churches, denominational tribes, and nations. Kevin and I often pray for other believers as we drive past churches. We pray for God's power, presence, blessings, and kingdom to break out in their midst.

If we pray all the *all*s in this passage, we will find ourselves praying more than ever, and we will see the power of Jesus overcome the work of the enemy in our lives, homes, communities, and world.

KEEP THE DOOR SHUT—TIGHT!

As we discern where the enemy is at work, we learn to lift up warfare prayers in the flow of an ordinary day. We are not paranoid, but we are always prepared to stand against the enemy. We are not superstitious, we are not substitious, we are soldiers. This means we are on guard, prepared, and ready to fight.

There is a simple little acronym that is often used in recovery groups to help people be ready to fight against moments of temptation. Since we know who the tempter is, we can use this tool to sharpen our thinking and prepare our hearts for battle. The word is HALT. Each letter represents a word and idea that reminds us about times the enemy is more prone to attack with lies, enticements, and temptations. Our job is to be prepared and ready to fight back.

My husband and I wrote a small-group curriculum with Robert Morris, a pastor from Texas who teaches on spiritual warfare. In his book *Truly Free*, he writes about how a person would lock their house up tight if they knew that a burglar was just outside. No one would leave a door slightly open in a situation when they knew someone was planning to rob them. As believers, we have an enemy who is a robber, a liar, a deceiver, and a prowling lion. With this in mind, we should shut and lock every door that might offer a point of entry into our lives. Here are four times that we can accidentally leave a door open. These four words spell the acronym HALT!

*Beware when you are **hungry***. When you have pushed hard and poured out, and your body is weary with physical hunger, be careful. This is a time when the enemy can come and entice you to fill yourself with something that promises to satisfy. All kinds of temptations can be launched in these moments. This was the tactic the enemy used with Jesus in the wilderness when he had fasted and was hungry (Matt. 4:1–4). When you face physical hunger, fill your body with healthy food and don't fall for the temptation to "satisfy" yourself with things that don't truly satisfy.

*Beware when you are **angry***. Anger can become a springboard for all kinds of temptations, and the enemy would love to launch you into actions, words, and behaviors that could have lasting negative effects on your life and relationships. The apostle Paul warns us, "'In your anger do not sin': Do not let the sun go down while you are still angry, and do not give the devil a foothold" (Eph. 4:26–27). When we live with unresolved anger and let it poison our lives, the enemy gets a foothold. We need to be aware of this and deal with our anger in a godly way.

*Beware when you are **lonely**.* Loneliness in our world is a growing epidemic. Even with all kinds of connections, contact, virtual friends, and group gatherings, we can still find ourselves feeling lonely. We must be aware that times of loneliness can become a place where the enemy can tempt us to fill ourselves with unhealthy relationships, substances, or activities. In these times we should recognize our need for genuine Christian community and the value of being an active part of the body of Christ.

*Beware when you are **tired**.* Fatigue and exhaustion are fertile ground for poor choices. The enemy sees when we are weary and knows our defenses can be down. We need to care for our bodies, get good sleep, and stay fresh. This is a spiritual discipline that will help us in the battle. I love the book *The Good and Beautiful God* by James Bryan Smith. I have used it as a discipleship resource as I have mentored many women and members of our church staff. It is the first in a three-book set called the Apprentice Series. The first exercise James offers to help Christians grow in spiritual maturity surprised me. To sum it up, it is about checking our sleep patterns and making sure we are well rested. I thought it would be something lofty like Bible study or passionate prayer. Instead, it was about getting good physical rest. What a simple reminder of the importance of watching our personal gauges and being sure we are refreshed.

IT IS NOT A FAIR FIGHT ANYMORE!

Gary Thomas, a wonderful pastor and writer, was visiting our church to preach and lead a seminar on his book *Sacred Parenting*. One of the many things he said that struck me was, "It is not a fair fight anymore." He was talking about how children and young people are exposed to sexual images and content at such an early age through online connections, cable channels, and the staggering availability of pornography. In the past, people had to go find this content, purchase it, and keep it hidden. Now, with a swipe and a few clicks, our phones, tablets, computers, and TVs have become portals to a world of temptation. The fight has changed and it is not fair.

The truth is, when it comes to spiritual warfare, it has never been a fair fight. Satan has no rules, no boundaries, and no conscience. He delights in the ruin of lives, the destruction of marriages, the collapse of churches, the end of friendships, the demise of families—any devastation he can bring.

The good news is we follow and serve a God who has power beyond our imagination. He is greater than the enemy of our souls. We follow a God who can prepare a young shepherd boy to bring down a Goliath (1 Sam. 17); our God can empower an Elijah to stand in victory over 850 false prophets (1 Kings 18); as God's people march in obedience, the walls of Jericho fall (Josh. 6); when God is present, the Red Sea parts (Ex. 13–15); in the power of God, the dead rise and sin is conquered (Matt. 28; 1 Cor. 15).

I suppose, when I really think about it, in an ultimate sense, it is *not* a fair fight. God is sovereign. He rules the universe. Christ has broken the back of Satan. Christ is risen! The Holy Spirit is present in our lives. Our God always wins!

YOUR PRAYER JOURNEY

Commit to lift up a protection prayer for a person you love. Identify where you feel the enemy is attacking and pray against the devil's tactics, in the name of Jesus, every time you think of this person. As you pray, reflect on the Bible passages from this chapter that assure you of the presence of God in your life and the power of God over the enemy. Ask God to show you the places in your life where you have left a door open for the enemy to slip a foot in. As the Holy Spirit reveals these areas, confess them. Pray for the power of God to shut these doors so you can walk in new levels of holiness and obedience.

Chapter Twelve

REPLACE WORRY WITH PRAYER

Prayer is an exchange. We leave our burdens,
worries, and sin in the hands of God. We come away
with the oil of joy and the garment of praise.
—F. B. Meyer

FOR ALMOST FOUR DECADES I was a runner. I met God as I ran. I prayed with my eyes open as I ran through spring rainstorms, hot and muggy Michigan summer days, pristine fall days with leaves crunching underfoot, and even freshly fallen snow. I drank in God's beauty and glory with each stride, and God spoke to me in powerful ways.

Then, with heartbreaking abruptness, my running came to an end. Back pain, neck problems, and a spinal surgery stopped my daily runs. One of the primary activities that connected me to God was no longer an option for me. I still miss it.

In an effort to find a new way to exercise and be outside, I took up swimming. Low-impact and less-jarring movement was just what the doctor ordered—literally. I went shopping for earplugs, a swim cap, and my first pair of goggles. Since this swimming thing was all new to me, I put on the goggles as tight as I could to assure myself that no water would get in. My goggles ended up leaving strange-looking indentations around my eyes for hours after I got out of the pool. Eventually I got the technical issues figured out, loosened my goggles a bit, and stopped disfiguring my face every time I swam.

When I wear my goggles, the water is crystal clear. I can see everything. Occasionally, I forget to bring them, and when I do, it is an entirely different experience. I can't open my eyes for very long because of the chlorine, and when I do open them, everything is blurry. My depth perception is off. It takes away the fun, and swimming is a lot less enjoyable.

Organic prayer is like swimming with a good pair of goggles. When we go through each day ready to pray at any moment, we are more aware of God's presence and power at work. We are more in tune with our environment, knowing how to interact with what is going on around us by praying more. The things that seem out of focus become clearer. We learn that prayer is not about a specific posture, place, or pattern of words. It is something we can do all through our day, no matter what we are involved in. We get a clearer vision of how God wants us to live with him, like him, and for him.

PRAYER AND WORRY

Because I have good goggles and have learned how to use them, I can swim with my eyes wide open. I pray as I swim. I pray for family members and friends as I do my laps. I lift up prayers for people in our church and in my community who are hurting. I praise and worship the God who loves us with everlasting love.

One morning, I woke up thinking about a situation in the life of a loved one. I was burdened and worried for this person. I went to the pool to do laps. My goggles were in place, my eyes wide open, so I launched into prayer.

After several laps I realized I was still praying for this same concern. At first I thought, "Wow, I really spent a lot of time praying for this one need." Then the Holy Spirit gently spoke this truth into my heart: *You have shifted from prayer to worry.* It was a shocking wake-up call because it was true. It was a hard but important moment in my prayer life.

Prayer and worry are radically different. But there are times when I think I am praying and I am actually reciting my worries to God rather than giving them over to him. When we take our pattern of worry, talk to God about it, and seek to justify our anxiety, we miss the opportunity to pray about our worry and find peace. Since I have identified this pattern in myself, I have tried to learn how to move from worry to prayer.

- When I worry, I bring my concerns, my fears, and my anxieties to God and recite them before him. Then I keep them for myself and continue on in my worry. When I am engaged in prayer, I seek to bring these things to God and leave them at his feet, trusting him to deal with them.

- When I worry, I am focused and fixated on the burden or problem I am facing. Authentic prayer turns my mind off the anxiety-producing situation and locks my attention on the God who has all power to overcome what I am facing.

- When I worry, I stay wound up and anxious. When I lift up

genuine prayers, I find peace and my heart is calmed because I know God has heard me and he cares.

For everyone who deals with worry and anxiety, there is a better way to live. God offers a path of peace that comes through prayer. To walk this path, we must commit to take a faith-growing journey that will help us replace our worry with prayer.

MY JOURNEY

During my son Zach's college years, he and his buddy Steve had an opportunity to travel to New Zealand for a month. He was excited to hike some of the trails and terrain of that beautiful country. Zach was thrilled about the adventure, but I can't say I was. I found myself worrying, a lot! I have a mother's heart, and no matter how old my sons are, I will always be, as they affectionately call me, their "Momma."

I have to be honest. I am often tempted to worry rather than pray. I know this is not healthy or helpful, but I am very good at worrying. It comes naturally! I have spent years trying to pray when I find myself anxious or worried about something or someone I love. So when my firstborn son told me he was getting on a plane and traveling to the other side of the planet for a month, I was profoundly aware that I needed some supernatural help to make it through.

I remember waking up on the morning before Zach was to embark on this great adventure. None of my sons had ever traveled so far away and for so long, so this was new territory for me. I found myself thinking, *I can't wait until this month is over and Zach is home safe and sound.* As this thought flashed through my mind,

I felt a gut-wrenching conviction. I was wishing my month away. Before Zach had even left, I was already worrying about the next thirty days. I knew this was not God's plan.

I asked myself, "Sherry, what kind of faith do you have?"

In that moment I knew I had to bring my concerns before the Lord. I needed to exchange my worry for prayer. So I prayed about my anxiety. Over the next couple of days I brought my worry to God and tried to place it in his capable and all-powerful hands. Unfortunately, I left many of those times of prayer carrying the same burdens with me. I did not lay them before God. I did not put my trust in him. I failed to surrender my son to his heavenly Father. I simply spent a lot of time worrying before God. My prayers were really a spiritualized form of anxiety, or what I call "worry prayers." Something needed to change.

As Zach began his trip on the other side of the globe, hiking and scaling rugged terrain far from our family, I began my own climb. The Lord moved me to reflect and meditate on Philippians 4:4–7: "Rejoice in the Lord always. I will say it again: Rejoice! Let your gentleness be evident to all. The Lord is near. Do not be anxious about anything, but in every situation, by prayer and petition, with thanksgiving, present your requests to God. And the peace of God, which transcends all understanding, will guard your hearts and your minds in Christ Jesus."

Of course I was familiar with this passage. I knew the basic message, but it did not control my heart and shape my mental outlook. I was praying with my eyes closed to the staggering truth of these Spirit-infused words. I was not praying with my eyes, ears, heart, and life wide open to God's presence, power, and goodness.

I wanted the "peace of God" to fill me. God wanted me to know that he was ready to guard my heart and change my way of thinking. This would be the precursor to being saturated with peace beyond my understanding.

WITH THANKSGIVING

In desperation, I got real honest with God and prayed, "Lord, please help me release my worry and anxiety. Teach me to give my son to you, even when it feels painful and unnatural." As I prayed, the Lord put a specific line on my heart: *Worrying will not help one single bit.* The truth of Philippians 4:4–7 started to come alive in my soul. Worrying would not help, but prayer, trust-filled prayer, would make a difference. From that moment on, every time I started worrying about Zach—and that was quite often at first—I would seek to exchange it for authentic prayer. Worry would not help one single bit, but prayer would.

I read the passage again and again, seeking to live out all the truth of the Scriptures. Then, as though a veil was lifted from my eyes and mind, I read two words I had seen before but not fully understood. It was a parenthetical thought that had been right there in the passage for almost two thousand years. At that moment it jumped off the page, captured my heart, and has been changing me ever since. These two words, and my effort to live them out with passion and devotion, have launched me on a continual journey of exchanging worry for prayer.

"With thanksgiving."

We must always be thankful when we pray. Prior to the clear exhortation of Philippians 4:6, verse 5 reminds us that the Lord is near. You can pray and avoid anxiety because the God of the universe is near you, ready to help you anytime, anywhere. As the psalmist declares in Psalm 120:1, "I call on the LORD in my distress, and he answers me."

We must recognize that God is in charge of all things. He rules the world, and he can take care of our lives and those we love. This is not a guarantee that everything will go our way. It is not a promise that life will be painless. For me at that moment it was a realization that my world-traveling son actually could end up in harm's way. But my worry would do nothing to help him—absolutely nothing! God, on the other hand, not only is near my son but also is able to deliver, protect, and help. Faithful and passionate prayer to the God who is near has power to guard and guide him.

I began to add thanksgiving to each of my prayers. I expressed thanks for my son, for his health, and for his friend Steve, who is a sensible and Jesus-loving man. I thanked God for Lloyd and Jan, sweet friends who live in New Zealand, who offered to make their home a staging point for Zach and Steve's adventures. I thanked God that Zach was a person who made wise decisions.

Through the flow of the remaining thirty days, I thanked God over and over again as I asked him to take care of my son: *Thank you, God, that I can come to you in prayer and trust you. Thank you that Zach and Steve rented a car instead of hiking everywhere. I give you thanks that you are on the throne at all times and in all places, even on the other side of the planet.* When worry would sneak in stealthily or come rushing into my heart and mind screaming for my attention, I would pray: *Please watch over Zach and Steve. Thank you that the guys have enough money to make it home. I lift up thanks that Zach has a phone in case of an emergency. Thank you that you rule every inch of this planet!* When doubts and anxiety would try to slip a foot in the door of my life and move back in, I would pray: *Thank you that you love Zach more than I do.* I kept lifting up prayers of thanks and trust to the God who placed my son in my arms and sent his only Son to save lost and broken people. *Lord, I continue to ask for your care over my son. I thank you that Zach has placed his faith and life in your hands. He is washed clean of all sin. Jesus is his Savior. If Zach does not come home, I know with unbending faith that heaven is his true home.*

Some years after learning this prayer lesson, I had the privilege of writing a small-group study with Ann Voskamp based on her book *One Thousand Gifts*. In this book and small-group study, Ann calls God's people to relentlessly, joyfully, and creatively make an ongoing list of "one thousand gifts" God has given them. This is a call to intentional and persistent thankfulness. These kinds of practices teach us that thankfulness is one of the keys to overcome the power of worry.

I made it through that month and my son Zach came home safely and full of fascinating stories. As the years have passed, I have prayed for Zach many more times, because New Zealand was the first of many traveling adventures. He was changed through this first experience and so was I. I realized, in the depths of my soul, that worrying does not help one single bit. On the other hand, prayer "with thanksgiving" makes all the difference in the world.

TRUST

The question is not whether we will face times of stress and worry-producing moments in life. We will. The real question is, Will we trust God no matter what we face? Praying with our hearts wide open is about understanding that we can trust God in the midst of everything we encounter in this life. The writer of Proverbs puts it this way:

Trust in the LORD with all your heart
and lean not on your own understanding;
in all your ways submit to him,
and he will make your paths straight.

—Proverbs 3:5-6

Over and over in the Bible we are assured that the God we worship is trustworthy, in the very core of his being. Isaiah tells us that "he tends his flock like a shepherd: He gathers the lambs in his arms and carries them close to his heart; he gently leads those that have young" (Isa. 40:11). We can trust God as the Good Shepherd of our lives and souls. The psalmist reinforces this when he writes,

Come, let us bow down in worship,
let us kneel before the LORD our Maker;
for he is our God
and we are the people of his pasture,
the flock under his care.

—Psalm 95:6-7

We can trust in this God with confident certainty. We don't have to be ruled by anxiety.

In Proverbs we are warned that we should never lean on our own understanding (Prov. 3:5). Worry, in a strange way, is a declaration that we don't trust God but are leaning on our own strength and ability to navigate hard times. When we worry in front of God and keep our burdens on ourselves, we are acting like we can handle these things better than he can.

Proverbs instructs us to follow the way of wisdom and acknowledge God in all our ways. This means we admit we can't fix our messes, overcome our anxieties, or worry away our worries. Instead, we place our trust in the Lord and give him our burdens.

TRADE

In the book of Isaiah we are called to trade a lie for the truth. I encourage you to read this passage (at least twice) very slowly. If you are in a place where you can do so, read it out loud. Ask yourself this question: What or who is being carried? Don't respond too quickly. There is more than one answer.

> Listen to me, you descendants of Jacob,
>> all the remnant of the people of Israel,
> you whom I have upheld since your birth,
>> and have carried since you were born.
> Even to your old age and gray hairs
>> I am he, I am he who will sustain you.
> I have made you and I will carry you;
>> I will sustain you and I will rescue you.
>
> With whom will you compare me or count me equal?
>> To whom will you liken me that we may be
>>> compared?
> Some pour out gold from their bags
>> and weigh out silver on the scales;
> they hire a goldsmith to make it into a god,
>> and they bow down and worship it.
> They lift it to their shoulders and carry it;
>> they set it up in its place, and there it stands.
>> From that spot it cannot move.

Even though someone cries out to it, it cannot answer;
it cannot save them from their troubles.

—Isaiah 46:3-7

There are two contrasting and shocking pictures being painted in this passage. I had read this Scripture many times through the years before it came into focus and struck my heart. The first picture is of a God who carries us.

Look at the passage. Let it touch you deeply and strengthen your trust in the God who loves you. From birth to old age, God carries his beloved people. He has carried you from before you were aware, before you could walk. He will carry you when you can no longer move in your own power. The God we worship is powerful and present, even when we don't recognize it. He rescues us, and his love for us is incomparable. When we recognize this God as our God, we can lay our burdens and worries at his feet. We can pray to this God with confidence.

In the passage there is also another, radically different picture. There are people who make their own god. They take gold and silver and fashion an idol. They try to place trust in this human invention, but it has no breath, no power, no life, and no love. These people lift their false god onto their own shoulders and carry it. Their god becomes a burden they must transport from place to place. They can't really pray to a god like this or trust an idol to protect and deliver them.

Praying with our hearts wide open is knowing the God we worship, the one who made us and carries us. He can be trusted because he is present and powerful. When we reduce God to a human invention or a mere idol, then we must carry him. When this happens, we are not trusting God to deliver, protect, or save us. What he wants is for us to lay down all idols and trade them for himself, the one who promises to carry us, no matter what we face.

The antidote to worrying can be found in living out the exhortation of Philippians 4. When we pray "with thanksgiving," our eyes turn to God and our thinking changes, and that in turn affects our hearts. Our eyes are fixed on God's faithfulness and power. When we trust in God and not our own understanding, he guides our path. When we trade powerless idols for the true God who carries us from the womb to the final days of this life, our confidence grows. Worry dies and faith is given new birth.

YOUR PRAYER JOURNEY

Root worry out of your prayer life. Bring an area of your life that tends to cause anxiety before the Lord in prayer. Flood this situation or concern with thanksgiving. Reflect on all you can think of that leads you to be thankful, and let these thoughts rule your heart and prayers. Then think about the many ways God has been present, powerful, and trustworthy in this area of your life. Every time you feel worry pop up in your heart or your prayers, battle it with declarations of thankfulness and trust.

Part Four

PRAYING WITH
LIVES WIDE OPEN

WHEN WE PRAY with our lives wide open, we allow the Holy Spirit to transform our behavior, change our direction, and shape our daily decisions. As we do this, opportunities to communicate with God come flooding in with surprising regularity. We no longer "try to pray" or "work at praying more." Speaking to God and hearing from our Lord become the norm.

As our lives become a dialogue with God, we will naturally and organically find ourselves praying *for* others with consistency and *with* others with growing regularity. The little and inconsequential things become an occasion to talk with God, and the big things move us to conversation with the only one who can manage the universe and our lives.

Praying with our lives open to God will lead us to the undeniable conclusion that God hears our prayers, God delights to answer, and something happens every time we pray.

Chapter Thirteen

PRAYING FOR OTHERS

When I pray for another person, I am praying for
God to open my eyes so that I can see that person
as God does, and then enter into the stream of love
that God already directs toward that person.
—Philip Yancey

"I'LL BE PRAYING FOR YOU!" We have all said these words. We mean it when we make this promise. We really do.

Most of us have had times when we make a commitment to pray for another person and then it slips our mind. We are not trying to be thoughtless or uncaring. Most of the time we are completely sincere and serious when we assure another person that we will pray. We mean it. We plan to. But sometimes we just forget.

We bump into that person at the store or see them at church the next week and realize, "I never prayed." We might even shoot up a quick prayer when we see them, assuring ourselves that we can now tell them we had prayed for them.

If you have been a Christian for any length of time and believe in the power of prayer, you can identify with this scenario in some way. You believe in prayer. You are committed to pray for others. But sometimes you get distracted or forget to pray.

When I am with someone who needs prayer, I am working on being more intentional about praying for him or her in that very moment. First, I often ask, "May I take a moment and pray with you right now?" If they are agreeable, I will pray right there, sometimes with eyes closed and often with eyes wide open. We will think about the privilege and power of praying *with* people in the next chapter.

Second, I often assure people with these words: "I will be praying for you as the Lord brings you to mind." What is so beautiful is that as we grow in our understanding of a posture open to "pray continually," God brings people to our minds and hearts at just the right time and more often than we would remember on our own.

The night before I was developing this chapter of the book, God reminded me to pray for someone. I have a dear friend whose relationship is now counted in decades rather than years. She and her husband are going through a long-term and difficult challenge in life that includes physical pain, legal entanglements, and relational challenges. I haven't talked to this friend in months, but last night as I lay in bed trying to fall asleep, this couple was strongly on my heart and mind. I lifted them up in prayer, asking God to strengthen them. I made my request to God with the eyes of my heart wide open to their pain, need, and situation. I cried out to the God who loves them and asked for relief from the burden they have been carrying for a couple of years.

The truth is, it had been some time since they came to my heart. They live two thousand miles away, and I don't get those natural prayer prompters when I "bump into them" because they are so far away. But that night God moved me to pray. After interceding for them, I finally dozed off.

The next morning I woke up to a text from this particular friend. It can be months between our exchanging texts, but the very morning after I prayed for her late at night, she sent me a quick note, not about her situation, but because she needed a picture from me taken a few years back. I responded by telling her that God had placed her on my heart the night before and that I had prayed for her. She sent a text right back that started with one simple word: "WOW!" She went on to let me know that they were going into a meeting that very morning that proved to be an important one in this ongoing struggle, and she was so touched by my prayers. I communicated to her that normally I would have just prayed for her and not shared about the prompting, but because she had texted me, I wanted her to be aware of what I felt was a tangible way God was encouraging her and letting her know that he is there for her during this difficult time. She was encouraged and strengthened. I believe God wanted to do that through this prayer for her. Every time we pray for someone, heavenly power is unleashed, God is present, miracles can happen, and we bring a real person into the throne room of God.

WHEN WE PRAY FOR OTHERS, WE ARE BEING FAITHFUL TO SCRIPTURE

All throughout the Bible the people of God have prayed. Confession, praise, thanksgiving, lament, and a host of other kinds of prayer are lifted from the hearts and lips of God's people. All true prayer is directed to God and inspired by the Holy Spirit.

Among all the ways we speak to God and listen for God is a

kind of prayer we call intercession. This is prayer lifted up for a person or situation. These prayers for others unleash the power of heaven and move the hand of God. It is not that we are seeking to pressure God to do something he is reluctant about. Instead, intercession is our way of joining with God on what he desires to do for the people in our lives that we care about.

Over and over the Bible calls us to intercede for others in prayer. We are told by the apostle Paul, "Devote yourselves to prayer, being watchful and thankful. And pray for us, too, that God may open a door for our message, so that we may proclaim the mystery of Christ, for which I am in chains" (Col. 4:2–3). James instructs followers of Jesus to "confess your sins to each other and pray for each other so that you may be healed. The prayer of a righteous person is powerful and effective" (James 5:16). Jesus calls us to pray for each other to have the daily bread we need (Matt. 6:11). Again and again the Bible invites and calls us to intercede for one another in prayer.

Intercession is unbounded. It is as great as human need and as wide as the planet we live on. We can pray for healing, for daily bread, for effectiveness in sharing faith, and for every other need we see as we walk through life. As you walk down the street, you can notice the needs around you and pray. As you drive around your community and see the brokenness, pray. Every time you intercede for anyone, you are following the call of God's Holy Word.

WHEN WE PRAY FOR OTHERS, WE BECOME MORE LIKE JESUS

Jesus was the great intercessor. In chapter 17 of John's gospel, we encounter what is sometimes called Jesus' High Priestly Prayer. Jesus was praying for his followers near the end of his life and ministry and he interceded for them. He asked for protection from the enemy and spiritual growth in their lives. This prayer of Jesus should inspire and teach us.

Next, our Savior turned his intercessory prayers to you and me. Jesus lifted up the people who would come to faith through the ministry of the first disciples. He was praying for us! Here is part of Jesus' intercessory prayer: "That all of them may be one, Father, just as you are in me and I am in you. May they also be in us so that the world may believe that you have sent me" (John 17:21). Unity and a common vision are the heart of Jesus, so he prayed for us to experience these realities.

The intercessory ministry of Jesus continues today. In Romans 8 we have this assurance: "Who then is the one who condemns? No one. Christ Jesus who died—more than that, who was raised to life—is at the right hand of God and is also interceding for us" (v. 34). The resurrected Savior is presently praying for us. What a reminder of how we become more like Jesus when we pray for one another! Whenever we lift up an intercessory prayer that is in line with the heart and will of Jesus, we are sharing in this ministry our Lord is still engaged in today.

When our three sons were quite young, we had a guest preacher named Ajith Fernando visit our church and bring the Sunday message. Ajith serves the church in his home country of Sri Lanka, and while he was at our church, Ajith stayed in our home and we became close friends in faith immediately. Ajith, his dear wife, Nelun, and their family have invested their lives serving the church through leading youth ministry, working with drug addicts, training leaders internationally, and writing some of the most insightful books of our generation. Over the past two decades God has bound our hearts together and made us one. Although we have spent time together only twice and have not seen each other face-to-face for more than two decades, we are family.

You might wonder how we could have such fondness for each other and feel so united over the miles and years. The answer is simple—we pray for each other. Hundreds of times over the past twenty years we have exchanged prayer needs and interceded for each other. In doing so, we have become more like Jesus, and our hearts have been united, even as Jesus prayed.

WHEN WE PRAY FOR OTHERS, WE ARE BEING THE CHURCH

A quick survey of the early church in the book of Acts paints a picture of a praying people. In almost every chapter you will find references to praying. They prayed for one another as a normal part of their community life. When there was a need, they lifted it up. This was not an occasional special prayer service; it was the flow of their lives as followers of Jesus, the Great Intercessor. When people were sick, they prayed. When a new mission was being started, they cried out to God for help and leading. When they needed wisdom, intercession was the normal response. Take time to read the book of Acts and take note of every time the people of God prayed for someone or something. This will propel you forward in your commitment to pray for others.

One morning as I woke up, I found myself thinking of my friend Betsy. I didn't really register it at first, but she came to my heart and mind a number of times through the day. I have learned that this is often a move of the Holy Spirit leading me to pray. I lifted Betsy up in prayer as I washed the dishes, did some other chores, and did my church work and my writing ministry. By the end of the day it struck me that I had prayed for my friend several times throughout the day. I sent her a text but didn't go into details. I just let her know that God had put her on my heart throughout the day and that I had prayed for her.

Betsy called me and said, "You have no idea how I needed your prayers today." She shared with me that a family member was in the hospital and she had been with them all day—it had clearly been a hard twenty-four hours for my friend. She was so grateful that I had been praying throughout the day. Betsy thanked me and said, "Sherry, it so encourages me to know that God was stirring you to pray and that he was letting me know that he cares." It struck me that we were being the church to each other.

As I thought about how God had showed love to Betsy through my prayers, my mind went to the previous Sunday. I had run into a friend I don't see very often. She caught me and said, "Sherry, something kind of interesting happened this past week. I couldn't get you off my heart and mind so I just kept praying for you." As she spoke those words, I found myself trying to hold back my tears. I told her that it had been a rough week. Knowing God had moved her to intercede for me meant more than she could possibly realize. I felt loved by her, but even more, I knew I was loved by my Father in heaven.

Every follower of Jesus has been filled with the very presence of God. The Holy Spirit dwells in us. He wants to move us to regular, natural, passionate prayer for one another. Be sensitive to God's leading. He will often direct you to pray for somebody. Pray for them and let them know that God inspired you to lift them up through intercession. This is one of the ways God grows us together as one body, the church, and continues to show his love toward us.

WHEN WE PRAY FOR OTHERS,
WE BECOME A CONDUIT
OF GOD'S POWER

As we walk with people who are facing situations beyond their means and capacity, we will be moved to pray. When we love people and want the best for them, we quickly recognize that our resources are limited at best and nonexistent in some situations. Pastor and writer Max Lucado puts it this way: "Intercessory prayer . . . acknowledges our inability and God's ability."[11] When we pray, we trust God to do what we could never accomplish.

The good news is that the power of God is beyond our comprehension and it can be unleashed as we intercede on behalf of others. Charles Stanley writes, "Our prayers are the link between God's inexhaustible resources and people's needs. . . . God is the source of power, but we are the instruments He uses to link the two together."[12] We do not pretend to think we have the power to meet all the needs we see, change lives, deliver from temptation, or set people free. But God's immeasurable resources can be unleashed through prayer.

Wes and Claudia planted and served Daybreak Church, a dynamic congregation in West Michigan, for many years. After feeling led to pray for Claudia a number of times over a few days, I checked in with her to see how she was doing. I simply let her know that the Lord had been bringing her to my heart and I had just been praying for her. I didn't really say much more. When Claudia realized that my heart was heavy for her, she later shared with me she had a sense that the Holy Spirit was moving her to be more diligent to check up on some physical concerns she was having about herself, and she felt the nudge from my prayers. When she went to the doctor, she asked them to do a thorough checkup. They soon discovered she had cancer and needed surgery.

Over the coming weeks, hundreds of people all over the world were interceding for Claudia and her family. God showed up in many ways. The family experienced the strength and comfort of the Holy Spirit. Claudia had the cancer removed and the doctors were amazed that it was localized and isolated.

Claudia and Wes wrote a letter to the many people who had been praying and assured us that they were confident God had done a miracle. The prayers of God's people unleashed the power of heaven, and their witness spoke of God's faithfulness to many non-believers that Wes and Claudia were seeking to point toward Jesus. When we pray, bodies can be healed, marriages can be restored, fractured friendships can be made whole, hearts can be opened to Jesus, hope can be restored, and countless other miracles can happen.

WHEN WE PRAY FOR OTHERS, WE ARE MOVED TO ACTION

Prayer is not passive. It is one of the most active things we will ever do. Not only does prayer unleash the power of heaven, it moves us. When we intercede in concert with the heart of God, we see the hand of God move and things happen. God may call us to enter into his ministry in the world. I can't begin to remember or list all the times I have been praying and have heard the gentle voice of the Spirit call me to do something.

All through the day God stirred me to pray for a wonderful young woman who is married to one of the pastors at our church. By the end of the day I felt I needed to call her and make myself available to serve in some way. My prayers called me to action. It just so happened that she was in the middle of a very busy time, and she said it would be helpful if I could come over and assist her in taking care of her kids for an afternoon. As we pray in line with God's heart, we should be ready to move into God-inspired action. This is a privilege and is the normal way of the Christian life.

WHEN WE PRAY FOR OTHERS, OUR SPIRITUAL LIFE IS EXPANDED

On a ministry trip in New Zealand, Kevin and I were doing some training with church leaders. One of the people in the meeting was a convert from another world religion, and he had been distanced from many of his own family members for almost three decades. We challenged all those present to intercede, pray, and seek ways to share their faith organically with the people God had placed in their lives. We encouraged them to be creative in their prayer lives for others, even using emails and text messages. We had no idea how this simple exhortation would expand the spiritual life of this one man.

A couple of days later, at another training time, he approached Kevin and me. With sadness in his eyes, he explained that he had tried to find a way to break into spiritual conversation with family members for more than thirty years and had hit roadblocks at every turn. I could feel his pain. Then his eyes brightened and he explained with joy that he had his first breakthrough.

After our last training time, the Holy Spirit put on his heart that he should text a short prayer to one of his relatives who he knew was going through a hard time. He followed that prompting and sent her a prayer. She responded with the words "Thank you," and then a very sweet text message.

This might not seem like a big deal to you or me, but for this man, after what felt like a lifetime of seeking to reach his family, it was a first positive step forward. His relative was open to his prayer and appreciative. God unleashed his presence and power and a door was opened to further conversation. Maybe one day this would lead to a conversation about God's sacrificial love for her. For this man, his whole spiritual life opened up when he took action and entered into intercessory prayer in a new way.

WHEN WE PRAY FOR OTHERS, THE GOSPEL SPREADS

Every conversion is born of a work of the Holy Spirit and the prayers of God's people. If you could track your spiritual legacy back through the heavenly realms, you would see that the prayers of God's people are an integral part of your story. For me, it was my parents and grandparents. Their prayers covered me from my mother's womb. For Kevin, it was the prayers of his Granny. It was also the relentless prayers of his sister Gretchen, who became a follower of Jesus a year before Kevin. In your story, there have been praying people who partnered with God on your journey to Jesus.

Our prayers can be God's way of sharing grace with other believers and the gospel of God's love with those who are still searching spiritually.

PRAYER REMINDERS

As we pray for others, there are a number of important reminders the Bible gives us. These are some of the things we can miss if we are not attentive and sensitive to God's direction as we pray. Here are five things I find helpful to remember. Each of these helps me keep my prayer life on track.

1. *Pray for people in places of authority.* God has put people in places of authority, and we are called to pray for them. Governmental leaders, law enforcement personnel, civic servants, and others in roles of influence should be covered with the prayers of God's people (1 Tim. 2:2). We can ask for wisdom and protection, for God's hand on their lives and families, and for the presence of Jesus to be revealed to them. We don't have to agree with someone to pray for them. Our prayers cross all boundaries to bring God into all situations.

2. *Cry out to God for those who are far from Jesus.* Our Savior called us to pray to the God of the harvest and ask him to send us out with the message and love of Jesus (Matt. 9:35–38). In the book of Acts, the prayers of God's people preceded the revival of Pentecost (chaps. 1–2). It is natural for most of us to pray for other believers. We should also be praying with fervor and consistency for the people in our lives who have not yet discovered that God loves them and that Jesus' sacrifice is enough to wash them clean of sin and begin a new life.

3. *Intercede for all of God's people.* We pray not only for the Christians close to us but for all of God's people (Eph. 6:18). Many churches pray for needs in their congregation. At Shoreline Church, where my husband and I serve on staff, we have a weekly practice. We pray for other local congregations. We actually call the other Christian churches in our community and ask, "What can we pray for you in our weekend services?" Each Sunday, as a congregation, we

pray for one church, for their lead pastor by name, and for specific needs and challenges they are facing. We are part of one body of Christ and believe praying for one another (as churches) is very important.

4. *Lift up the people who see themselves as your enemy.* Jesus called us to pray even for those who treat us badly and persecute us (Matt. 5:44). If you knew what the early church would face under Roman persecution in the first century, this exhortation would shock you. If first-century Christians could pray for those who were ravaging the church, destroying Christian communities, and martyring fellow believers, we can certainly pray for those who are hostile to us and our faith.

5. *Pray for God's will to be done.* When Jesus taught his followers how to pray, he told us to pray for his kingdom, not our own personal empires, to come. He directed us to pray, not for the fulfillment of our personal whims, but for his will to be done (Matt. 6:10). In all of our prayers for ourselves, for Christian friends, for nonbelievers, for governing authorities, and even for enemies, we are to pray for God's will to be done. If we can pray in God's will, then we can pray in the name of Jesus. When we pray in the name of Jesus, we can have confidence that God will hear and answer our prayers.

Compassion moved the heart of Jesus as he walked on this earth with his eyes wide open. He saw people wandering like sheep without a shepherd (Matt. 9:35–37). When Jesus looked at the masses of people who were headed into danger and far from his grace, he made a shocking declaration. He called people to prayer. Here are the words of Jesus in Matthew's gospel: "The harvest is plentiful but the workers are few. Ask the Lord of the harvest, therefore, to send out workers into his harvest field" (9:37–38).

When our eyes are open to see the needs all around us, we are moved to organic prayer. As we pray, we are propelled into action. There is a great harvest of souls that God wants to bring in. People are more open to the message of Jesus than we imagine. The problem is not with God. He has made a way for lost sheep to come home. The issue is with believers in Jesus. It is the workers that are few. Will you pray for the Lord of the harvest to move people out into our broken world with his love and grace? And will you be first in line to follow him on this mission every day of your life?

YOUR PRAYER JOURNEY

In the coming month, try doing a 1-1-1 prayer. This is something Lee Strobel taught at one of the Organic Outreach Conferences we held at Shoreline Church. The idea is simple. You pray for a person who is not yet a follower of Jesus. Commit to intercede for them and ask God to soften their heart, open them to the love of Jesus, and give opportunities for Christians (including you) to share the gospel of Jesus. Here is the 1-1-1 part: What you commit to do is set an alarm and reminder on your phone or watch for 1:00 p.m. every day. At this time, pray for this one person for one minute. That's it. Of course, if 1:00 p.m. is not the best time, you can adjust this. I found 9:00 p.m. to be the best time in my schedule for this prayer, so I call this prayer my 9-1-1 prayer. This is one way to remind ourselves to live a life open to "pray continually."

Chapter Fourteen

PRAYING WITH OTHERS

If we truly love people, we will desire for them
far more than it is within our power to give
them, and that will lead us to prayer.
—Richard Foster

IT WAS MY SOPHOMORE YEAR at Calvin University and I was terrified. I had been hired as a resident assistant for the young women in my dorm, and at the first leaders' meeting they told me to do something that made me question whether I could still be an RA. I did not know how I was going to do it. I went through moments of feeling nervous, anxious, and genuinely afraid.

You might be wondering what the leaders at this Christian university could have asked me to do that would paralyze me like this. What strange task had they requested of me? What mammoth expectation could they have heaped on me that would cause this level of concern?

They asked me to pray out loud with the girls on my floor.

I had grown up with praying parents. I was part of a praying church. I had been a person of prayer from my youngest days and memories. But praying out loud with others, aside from my parents, scared me more than I could put into words.

I finally talked with my roommate, Connie, the other resident assistant for our floor, and told her how I felt. I confessed my fear and the temptation to find some way out of this dilemma. Her response was as beautiful and sweet as her heart: "Sherry, why don't we just pray together every morning. You can practice with me. There won't be any pressure. We will just talk to God our Father together." For some reason, this felt safe, and I agreed. Morning after morning we prayed. We spoke to Jesus as a friend. We lifted up reverent prayers to the God who rules the universe. We thanked God for his blessings and praised him for his goodness.

Before I knew it, I had grown comfortable praying out loud with my friend. I still had a little nervousness, but most of it was gone. When the floor meeting happened and I had to lead this group of young women in prayer, I was able to do it. I must be honest, it was still a learning curve, but my comfort level grew stronger with time. There were little bouts with fear, but God gave me courage. As the semester went on, praying with the young women on my floor became quite natural.

I learned that talking to God with others could become a natural part of our lives, even when we start out being anxious about it. Since that time in college, praying with others has become more and more a part of my life. I have tried to help people learn to pray in community so they, too, can experience the joy, delight, and power of praying with others.

JESUS PRAYED WITH PEOPLE

Jesus was a beautiful example of living in a state of perpetual prayer. He certainly modeled the discipline of slipping away to private places for one-on-one times of communication with the Father (Mark 1:35). He also made a point of praying in community. In key times of his ministry Jesus would sometimes gather a small cluster of friends (often Peter, James, and John) and slip away for prayer. One time, before Jesus was transfigured, he asked these three friends to go away to the mountain and pray with him. It was in this time of prayer retreat with close brothers that the Father declared, "This is my Son, whom I have chosen; listen to him" (Luke 9:28–35). Jesus loved to talk with the Father in community with others.

When Jesus taught his followers to pray, he called them to do this in community. Have you ever noticed that the Lord's Prayer is a call to seek the face of God with other believers? In this well-known prayer, Jesus did not call us to pray "me and my." Instead, he taught his people to pray, "Our, us, and we!" Read this prayer out loud and emphasize the words in italics:

This, then, is how you should pray:

"*Our* Father in heaven,
hallowed be your name,
your kingdom come,
your will be done,
 on earth as it is in heaven.
Give *us* today *our* daily bread.
And forgive *us* our debts,

as *we* also have forgiven *our* debtors.

And lead *us* not into temptation,

but deliver *us* from the evil one."

—Matthew 6:9-13, emphases added

This does not mean that we shouldn't pray, "My Father in heaven." But it is clear that Jesus is teaching that praying with other believers in Christian community should be commonplace in our lives.

PRAYER WITH OTHERS SHOULD BE COMMON

Many followers of Jesus feel like I did when I found out that I had to pray out loud with the college girls in my dorm. Praying with others can cause fear, even for very committed and mature Christians. It can seem strange and out of place for those who have not done it regularly. This anxiety over praying with others can keep people from joining a small group, from accepting a leadership role in the church, and from growing close Christian friendships. I have met wonderful Christians through the years who live with a very real fear about praying in a group or one-on-one with other believers.

God's desire for you is to have rich and meaningful times of prayer one-on-one with him. He also delights when you pray with others in groups, and face-to-face with other Christians. If this comes naturally for you, wonderful! If this makes you nervous, you are in good company. Lots of us have had to grow, learn, and press through our fear until this became a common part of our lives. I encourage you to find one person you respect and trust as a brother or sister in Christ, like I did with my friend Connie, and practice praying out loud with that person. Make this a normal part of your life until you are ready to pray with other people.

I am so thankful that I pressed past my fears. Praying with others has become a rich and meaningful part of many of my relationships. At the end of a phone call I will sometimes pray with whomever I am talking with. After church services, people come to talk with me and I can end up praying with many of them. After they share a need or joy, I simply say, "Can we take a moment and pray together?" These times of prayer are sweet and filled with the presence of Jesus. They deepen our relationship. When I walk with friends in the hills near our home or at the beach, we often spend some of the time praying as we walk, with our eyes wide open. We move in and out of conversation with each other and conversation with God. It is not unusual to pray at multiple times during a longer walk with a friend or with my husband.

Prayer should become part of our connection with God and with the people in our lives. If we are learning to pray without ceasing, continually talking with God, we will find ourselves praying with others. Since much of life is in community with other people, the only way we can pray continually is to pray with others.

When prayer becomes part of the fabric of our relationships with family members, friends, neighbors, and the other people in our lives, we begin to encounter God in our relationships. Prayer is not just hidden away at home or reserved for bedtime or the blessing before a meal. It is engrafted in all we do. This is organic prayer! As we pray, God shows up; we encounter his presence, power, and glory in our relationships. The great Christian thinker A. W. Tozer wrote, "True Christian experience must always include a genuine encounter with God. Without this, religion is but a shadow, a reflection of reality, a cheap copy of an original once enjoyed by someone else of whom we have heard."[13] There is no better way to encounter God in our relational world than to pray together.

As we grow in organic prayer, we often find ourselves praying with other people more frequently. There is a special joy and connection that comes as we pray with other followers of Jesus. In addition, as prayer becomes a natural part of our lives, we can invite nonbelievers to pray with us. Both my husband Kevin and I have prayed many times with people who are not yet followers of the Savior, and these are amazing and powerful times when God draws near.

At first, this might seem strange. But you would be amazed at how many non-Christians are open to prayer. When you are in a conversation with someone who has experienced deep pain or is facing a challenge, you can offer to pray for that person right then and there. If someone shares a life-changing joy or some good news, you can say, "May I take a moment and thank God for [the birth of your child, your promotion, your spouse's successful surgery, or whatever good thing that has happened]?" Many people will say yes to an offer of prayer in those moments. I have found if I say, "I would be honored to pray for you right now, and we don't even have to close our eyes!" it is amazing how this raises people's interest and removes their anxiety. I often give a very brief explanation that the Bible never says we have to close our eyes or fold our hands when we pray. We can just talk to God like we talk to another person.

This can lead to a wonderful time of prayer. It can open the door for a conversation about prayer. And it can help the person realize that talking to God is not some super-spiritual exercise reserved for churches or cathedrals. It can happen anytime and anywhere—with eyes closed or eyes open. I have a number of people in my life who have not yet received Jesus as their Savior but are very open to prayer and will even share prayer needs with me when they are going through a hard time or celebrating something wonderful. These times with God in prayer are part of how God is drawing spiritually curious people to the heart of Jesus.

IDEAS AS YOU PRAY WITH OTHERS

There is no formula for how to pray. Jesus was clear that many of the people of his day had fallen into a bad practice of heaping up words and prayers that were vacant and empty of meaning (Matt. 6:7). He called his people to pray from their hearts, in community, and to focus on big themes that would guide their prayer lives (Matt. 6:9–13). But our Savior did not give an exact script for prayer. What he gave was a guideline to help us identify key themes and topics that should be lifted up regularly in our prayer lives.

With this in mind, we should beware of formulaic prayers and rigid structures. At the same time, there are several biblical and practical ideas that will help us move forward in how we pray with others.

Ask God to lead you by his Holy Spirit. Prayer should be an organic, natural part of our lives. It should also be supernatural. We should be led by the Holy Spirit of God in all we do. Ask God to help you notice good times to pray with others. Invite the Spirit to give you boldness and confidence to say, "Can we take a moment and pray about that?" Look for God-given moments that are natural for praying together.

Pray out of the depths of your relationships. Since prayer comes out of who we are, our prayers with others should reflect the depth and nuance of that relationship. When we have a close and intimate friendship or connection with a family member, our prayers will reflect this relationship and can go deep quickly. When we are first getting to know someone, our prayer might be less intense and vulnerable because the relationship is young. This is fine. It is to be expected. One of the wonderful benefits of praying with others is that it deepens our relationship with them as God grows our hearts together as his children.

Be sensitive to the setting and the time. I find there are moments when praying together out loud, with eyes closed or open, does not feel appropriate. This is not a matter of being ashamed or embarrassed. It is about wisdom. I have had servers at restaurants we often patronize share an honest pain or struggle, and I have wanted to pray for them but felt led by the Spirit to simply say, "I want you to know that I will be praying for you today about your situation." Having them stop in the middle of their work does not seem like the natural or right thing to do.

Some settings lend themselves to praying with eyes open more than closed. If I am going to have a time of prayer with someone in a public setting, I sometimes say, "Let's pray with our eyes open." I was meeting with a couple of friends at a coffee shop, one with long tables that place others very close to you. One of my friends was talking about a direction she felt God might be taking her. It was a very important moment and seemed like a great time to pray. I spent a few minutes sharing about praying with our eyes wide open and then invited my friends to pray. To any casual observer, they would have thought we were just talking. To God, it was clear we were praying. We simply invited the Lord of glory into the conversation and kept talking.

As often happens the first time I pray with eyes open with a friend, there was a little awkwardness. But it soon felt quite natural. We prayed for the Lord's leading, for wisdom, for clear direction. After we finished praying, both of my friends shared how good it felt to remember that God is with us and to pray in this new, old way of communicating with God.

Pray with people who are not yet followers of Jesus. When the opportunity presents itself, we find this very meaningful and rich. We had just landed in Kansas City and were standing at the baggage claim area when a gentleman came up to my husband and asked if this was the place to pick up luggage for our flight. He said yes, and they began to chat. Kevin asked him, "Are you coming home or leaving home?" He responded, "Kind of both." He went on to explain that he had grown up in the Kansas City area but now his home was on the West Coast. So coming to Kansas City always felt like coming home, even though he had a new home.

Kevin asked, "What brings you back to this area?" The gentleman got very serious as he said, "I just found out that my mom has stage-four cancer." He and Kevin talked for a few minutes, and two things became clear: this man was in need of prayer and was also a spiritual seeker. After hearing some of his story, Kevin asked, "Would you mind if I said a quick prayer for you and your mom as you go to visit with her?" It seemed totally natural and appropriate. The man seemed very touched and said, "I would love that."

Kevin explained that they did not need to bow their heads or close their eyes. He said, "I will lift up a prayer and you can just agree in your heart." After Kevin prayed, they went back to talking. Kevin was able to encourage him and learn more about his story. Before we parted ways, this gentleman asked Kevin, "Are you a pastor or something?" Kevin said, "Actually, I am, but I would have prayed for you even if I was not."

As I wrote earlier, both Kevin and I have prayed with nonbelievers more times than we can count. When we offer to pray, with eyes open or closed, they almost always say yes. Every time we pray, God shows up in a special way.

Don't force prayer. It is wonderful to offer prayer. It is a joy when people say yes. It is inappropriate to force the issue. So if someone is open to pray with you, wonderful. Pray. If someone is not ready, be gracious and patient. Let them know that you are always available to pray with them, but assure them that you will never press the issue.

Rejoice in the great work you see God do, and share each other's burdens. Kevin and I were driving from Auckland to Lake Taupo in New Zealand. We were speaking at a conference for pastors and church leaders from all over the country. The couple driving us, Harataki and Shona, were gracious and kind people. We had met them on two previous trips to New Zealand and had grown very fond of them but did not know them well. Now we had about four hours to really get to know one another.

As we began to share about our lives, I expressed a concern I was facing. Harataki continued the conversation by breaking into prayer with his eyes open because he was driving. Shona contributed to the conversation with God as well. Of course, I was smiling in the back seat because I was writing this book at the time, but I was also encouraged because of the depth of care they were giving me. They were asking God to move in power in my life. As we drove, they shared some of the joys and challenges they were facing in life, family, and ministry. They have a powerful passion for the people they seek to minister to, and as we drove, we continued on our prayer time for their ministry concerns. Over the next four hours we must have prayed half a dozen times. We never said, "Let's pray," or "Shall we stop to pray about that?" Prayer simply flowed naturally in the course of our conversation. The bond between us grew in this four-hour drive and prayer time as God wove our hearts together.

That drive was a powerful picture of sharing burdens as well as rejoicing together. Prayer is a natural way to express our hearts to God and to support each other. My hope and prayer for you is that regular and natural prayers will flow when you are with other people who know and love Jesus.

PRAYING WITH GROUPS OF PEOPLE

There are unique dynamics when a group of people prays together. This is a different experience from that of praying one-on-one. Here are some things to be sensitive to when praying in a group.

Pray from your heart. Authentic prayer comes from the depths of our souls. Don't be afraid to let your heart show through when you pray. God knows what is happening inside of you. Be honest in prayer, even when you are with others.

Keep your prayers brief. When you are praying with a group of people, it is always best to be brief with your prayers. You can pray numerous times, but if you go on for an extended time, others might feel they are not welcome to jump in and add their voices. Shorter prayers make room for many to lift their hearts before the Lord and for all those gathered to agree with an "Amen!"

Listen and engage. Don't spend your time planning your next prayer. Instead, you should listen to the prayers of others and engage your heart. Agree with them. Pray silently as others are praying out loud. Then jump in and add your prayer.

Build on the prayers of others. If a person has lifted up a prayer that connects with your heart, agree with their prayer and then build on it. You can pray, "Lord, I agree with Diane and her prayer for strength as she faces this time of loneliness and fear. I ask for your Holy Spirit to descend on her and grant her courage and a deep sense of your presence. Help her know she is never alone." When you listen well, you can be moved to pray in concert with others.

Use normal language. Be careful not to use overly spiritual or "churchy" language. When you are praying in a group, it is helpful to use ordinary language so others do not feel they have to mimic and copy super-spiritual-sounding prayers. Work to use conversational language that others can understand. No one should need a theological dictionary just to understand your prayer.

Confidentiality is essential. As you grow in praying in groups, know that some prayers will be surprisingly transparent and even vulnerable. It should be understood that whatever you pray about is private—between God and whoever is in your group. If prayers become fodder for gossip, this will cause people to shut down when they pray with you. Keep people's prayers in confidence, and God will draw more people to pray with you.

———

It is an honor to come into the presence of the Living God. It is a greater honor to know we can talk with him in prayer and that he hears us. This blessing is multiplied when we pray with others. Seek to make this a normal part of your daily life and see how God grows your faith in him and intimacy with the people he has placed in your life.

YOUR PRAYER JOURNEY

Identify a Christian friend or family member that you have never prayed with. Sometime in the coming week, look for an opportunity to pray with this person. When he or she shares a joy or sorrow, ask if you could pray about that together. If it seems appropriate, you might even want to share what you are learning about praying with your eyes wide open. A second challenge is to look for an opportunity to pray with someone who is not a Christian. If the door is open and you ask someone if you could pray together, be sure to say that you will be doing the praying (out loud) and this person can quietly agree in his or her heart. If you see this person regularly, be sure to follow up and ask if he or she has experienced some kind of answer to the prayer you lifted up together.

Chapter Fifteen

PRAYING FOR THE LITTLE AND BIG THINGS OF LIFE

We tend to use prayer as a last resort, but God wants it to be our first line of defense. We pray when there's nothing else we can do, but God wants us to pray before we do anything at all.
—Oswald Chambers

MOST OF US have had the privilege of meeting a person who has a prayer life so natural that he or she gets dubbed a "prayer warrior." I heard this term occasionally as a girl growing up in and around the church. Of course, people like this don't have a name tag that says "Prayer Warrior," and they are not given badges or medals to wear on a uniform. They are ordinary people who have faith in Jesus and are convicted that the power of God is unleashed through prayer. With this confidence, they pray often, talk to God with passion, and see wonderful answers to prayer.

I met such a person when God brought Alma into my life. What struck me about this humble woman was that she seemed to pray naturally about everything. It did not matter how big or small it was. Alma prayed.

I first encountered Alma when Kevin and I accepted an invitation to speak for a church leaders' conference. The Christian Reformed Church of Australia held a national event for pastors, church leaders, and spouses every two years. This particular year they based their conference on one of my husband's books, *Leadership from the Inside Out.*

Alma was one of the leaders at this conference, and during one of the many sessions Kevin and I led on this topic about the inner life of a Christian leader, she felt a nudge in her heart to begin lifting up a very specific prayer. Her prayer was that someday, if she had the opportunity, she would invite me to be the speaker for their denominational biennial women's gathering. In her heart, this was a big prayer. Would she have influence to help make this happen? Would I be available? Could they afford to bring someone from the other side of the planet over for this event? There were lots of questions and many possible obstacles, but Alma prayed and carried it to the Lord.

About four years later, Alma's opportunity to help find a speaker came and she contacted me. Alma shared about the women's conference and asked me to pray with her to seek the Lord's direction about my coming to speak at this four-day event. As we prayed, I felt a clear prompting from the Holy Spirit that I was to join the team she was leading to minister to this national gathering of women.

Over the following several months, Alma and I talked over the phone and planned regularly. We prayed every time we communicated. We prayed for the conference, and then Alma would pray for my family members by name. I loved how she wove prayer into the natural flow of her life and ministry.

When I arrived in Adelaide, Australia, it was Alma who met me at the airport and hosted me. Our hearts had already been bound together in ministry partnership and through our times of praying together. In the coming days we became sisters. I already knew Alma prayed about the big things. Now I would discover how passionately and effectively she prayed about little things.

KOALA PRAYERS

Early on in our time together Alma told me that she really hoped and prayed that the time at her house before the conference would refresh me. She told me later it was her prayer not only that I would be refreshed but that I would get a chance to see a koala while I was there. These shy creatures sleep a lot and often in the daytime. There are people who live in Australia who have never seen one outside a zoo. Alma really wanted me to see a koala.

It might seem like a small and silly prayer to some people. But Alma wanted me to have a sweet experience while in Australia, and she thought it would be nice for me to see some Australian wildlife. Alma believes God cares about the big things and also the smallest of things, so she prays for everything.

My first day in Adelaide, Alma took me on a two-hour walk in a beautiful park. After walking and talking for a bit, Alma said, "I apologize that I keep looking up as we walk, but I am looking for a koala. I would love for you to see one." She was matching her prayer with effort. I told her I hadn't really noticed but was touched that she was going to such lengths for me to see a koala. We finished the walk without any sign of one.

As we drove to the retreat center, we passed through the eastern suburbs on the way to Belair, where the conference would be held. As we paused at an intersection, I got a tickle in my throat and began coughing and could not stop. Alma said, "That's strange, I wonder if there is something in the air." She looked up into the trees, to see if something there was the cause of my throat irritation, and smiled. "Sherry, look up, there is a koala in that tree." Sure enough, after two hours looking for a koala in a park, God surprised us with one, though in an unexpected place.

As we drove on, we laughed and delighted in how God drew our attention to see a koala through a tickle in my throat. In that moment, I experienced a sweet touch of God's love as I realized he had both answered Alma's prayer and provided a koala for me to see in a surprising and fun way. Through praying for big things, God led me to Australia to teach his Word. Through praying for small things, I got to see a koala and have a special moment with a dear sister in Christ.

A PSALM FOR BIG AND SMALL THINGS

I love the book of Psalms. This prayer book of God's people leads us to speak with God about the simple delights of life and the times we walk through the valley of the shadow of death. All through the Psalms we learn that both the big and small needs we have matter to God. In Psalm 103 we see this truth in a vivid way. Read this psalm and reflect on what it might lead you to pray about:

> Praise the LORD, my soul;
>> all my inmost being, praise his holy name.
> Praise the LORD, my soul,

and forget not all his benefits—
who forgives all your sins
and heals all your diseases,
who redeems your life from the pit
and crowns you with love and compassion,
who satisfies your desires with good things
so that your youth is renewed like the eagle's. . . .

For as high as the heavens are above the earth,
so great is his love for those who fear him;
as far as the east is from the west,
so far has he removed our transgressions
from us.

As a father has compassion on his children,
so the LORD has compassion on those who
fear him;
for he knows how we are formed,
he remembers that we are dust.

—verses 1–5, 11–14

God knows us. He is our ever-present and powerful provider. This psalm teaches us to be sure we don't forget "all his benefits."

What benefits has God given you? They are countless and range from the delight of a sparrow landing on a windowsill to the sacrifice of his only beloved Son. God's benefits are small and big.

Our God satisfies us. Each breath of air is his gift. The provision of a job. Good friends. A great meal. A sunny day. God satisfies us with small and big things. Our prayers should reflect the God who meets our needs, gives us benefits, heals our hurts, and forgives our sins.

I love how the Apostles' Creed reminds us that God is intimate and present. It also declares that our God is sovereign and Ruler of the universe. The creed begins like this: "I believe in God the Father Almighty, maker of heaven and earth." God is our Father. He cares about the smallest and most intimate of needs and concerns. God is also almighty. He has the power to do something about the situations we face. We pray to the God who is both Father and Almighty. Personally, I like that "Father" comes before "Almighty" in this creed.

If you are a parent, you know that you always want your children to come to you with whatever is on their hearts, no matter how big or small. How sad it would be for a loving parent to find out that their child had needed help but hadn't asked for it. In the same way, God wants his children to approach him with confidence and faith. Our part is to ask. God's part is to decide how to answer our prayers in his sovereign wisdom.

TOO LITTLE OR TOO MUCH?

Some years ago, when our sons were young, our dear friend Ben Patterson came to preach at our church. Ben is a man of prayer who, along with his wife, Lauretta, has had a powerful impact on both Kevin and me. While Ben was preaching, he looked at the congregation and asked us a question.

"Do we ask too much of God, or too little?"

One of my boys leaned over and said, "Too much!"

Ben went on to say that he believed we do not ask enough of God. He quoted from *The Weight of Glory*, where C. S. Lewis wrote, "It would seem that Our Lord finds our desires not too strong, but too weak. We are half-hearted creatures, fooling about with drink and sex and ambition when infinite joy is offered us, like an ignorant child who wants to go on making mud pies in a slum because he cannot imagine what is meant by the offer of a holiday at the sea. We are far too easily pleased."[14]

Though many of us, like my son, might think we ask too much of God, the truth is that most of us should ask more of the Creator and Sustainer of the universe. He cares about our deepest dreams, pain, fears, and longings. He also cares about the smallest details of our lives. The God who made the heavens and the earth also knows the number of hairs on our heads and when a sparrow falls from the sky. He cares about all of our lives and wants us to bring everything to him in prayer.

OPEN WIDE YOUR MOUTH

I often begin a conference or a longer speaking engagement with a simple picture from Psalm 81:10:

> I am the LORD your God,
>> who brought you up out of Egypt.
> Open wide your mouth and I will fill it.

The words that have caught my attention and given me a vivid picture of prayer are "Open wide your mouth." This passage sends a message that God is ready to fill us. The real question is, Will we open our mouths, our hearts, and our lives to receive all he is ready to give?

At conferences I will often invite someone who loves M&M's to come forward and join me up front. I explain to them that I would love to give them some M&M's and ask them to prepare to receive the M&M's I want to give. I have a large bag with me, more than their two hands can hold.

Each time, the person will cup their hands together, turn them upward, and seek to make as much space as they can for maximum M&M receiving. I begin pouring M&M's into their hands—as much as they can hold. I remind those listening that I will give this person as much as they can handle, and I do. I fill their hands until they can't hold one more M&M.

This picture communicates a message. God wants us to open our mouths, our hands, our hearts, and our lives to receive more. This is not about self-serving childish requests. It is about God wanting to give us so many benefits that we will never forget how good he is. It is about a heavenly Father who truly is almighty and has more to pour into us than we can possibly handle. Our part is to open wide so God can fill us. Prayer is one of the best ways to open up and receive from God.

Ask more of God. Expect more of God. Seek him for the biggest of things and the "impossible" things. And ask him for the little stuff—he really does care about the smallest details of your life.

At one event where I was speaking, I read Psalm 81:10 and invited a woman forward to receive as many M&M's as she could handle. I wanted these beloved children of God to get the message and open their mouths wide to receive from the Lord. When I lifted up the jumbo pack of M&M's and told her to take a posture of receiving, she did *not* open her hands or turn them upward. She surprised me by grabbing the edges of her long T-shirt and carefully making it into a bowl for her M&M's.

I smiled. I poured. The crowd cheered and laughed. She walked away with *all* of my M&M's.

HOW LITTLE IS TOO LITTLE?

As we learn to ask more of God, we will discover that praying all through our day will lead us to pray about many things that seem small and even inconsequential. When someone races up behind us while we are driving and follows way too close, we can pray for them and let them pass instead of getting upset and reciprocating with road frustration. When we find ourselves in a situation that seems to be beyond our wisdom, we will reflexively ask for heavenly insight. When a situation seems tense, we pray for the peace of the Holy Spirit. Nothing is too small or mundane to bring before the Lord.

There is a wonderful story I heard years ago about a little boy praying for ice cream. I am not sure of the original source, but the message is memorable and the story worth retelling:

> Last week, I took my children to a restaurant. My six-year-old son asked if he could say grace. As we bowed our heads he said, "God is good. God is great. Thank you for the food, and I would even thank you more if Mom gets us ice cream for dessert. And liberty and justice for all! Amen!"
>
> Along with the laughter from the other customers nearby, I heard a woman remark, "That's what's wrong with this country. Kids today don't even know how to pray. Asking God for ice cream! Why, I never!"
>
> Hearing this, my son burst into tears and asked me, "Did I do it wrong? Is God mad at me?" As I held him and assured him that he had done a terrific job and God was certainly not mad at him, an elderly gentleman approached the table. He winked at my son and said, "I happen to know that God thought that was a great prayer."
>
> "Really?" my son asked.

"Cross my heart," the man replied. Then in a theatrical whisper, he added (indicating the woman whose remark had started this whole thing), "Too bad she never asked God for ice cream. A little ice cream is good for the soul sometimes."

Naturally, I bought my kids ice cream at the end of the meal. My son stared at his for a moment and then did something I will remember the rest of my life.

He picked up his sundae and without a word, walked over and placed it in front of the woman. With a big smile he told her, "Here, this is for you. Ice cream is good for the soul sometimes; and my soul is good already."[15]

The point is not that we need to pray for ice cream. The truth is, we can pray about everything, including ice cream.

A FRESH PERSPECTIVE AT SIX IN THE MORNING

My sister Dawn walked out of the house early one morning to water her flowers before the heat of the day set in. As she was finishing her task, she tried to open the front door to go back into her house when she realized she had mistakenly locked herself out. Frustrated for a moment, she had a glimmer of hope as she heard her husband pulling out of the driveway and turning the corner to head to work. She tried to wave him down, but unfortunately, he assumed she was waving goodbye for the day. Frustrated again at herself and now at her husband, and standing in her pajamas in front of her house, she realized this was not a good start to the day.

After checking all the doors and realizing she was truly locked out, she looked at her watch again. Her neighbor had a backup key, but she did not want to knock on her door before 7:00 a.m. As she shared with me later, it was at that moment the Holy Spirit reminded her of things we had been talking about—that she can pray continually about anything at any time. So she began to pray.

Over the next hour my sister Dawn met with Jesus. She first asked God to help her deal with the frustration of this experience, owning up to her mistake and realizing that her frustration toward her husband proved to be a little comical. As she sat enjoying the beautiful flowers blooming in her yard, she thanked God for them. She prayed for family members. Dawn talked to Jesus about life, big and small things. Instead of being frustrated for an hour, it became an opportunity to enjoy fellowship with God. At 7:00 a.m. she went to her neighbor and got her extra key and let herself back into the house. Prayer had changed the trajectory of her day. She called me later in the day to share what had happened. We talked and laughed together and celebrated all she was learning about discovering the presence and power of God in the everyday.

HOW BIG IS TOO BIG?

Nothing is too big for God's power. The one who spoke all creation into existence and sustains all things by his word is entirely capable of meeting any need we face. It is always right to come to our heavenly Father and ask for his help, protection, strength, and healing. He wants to hear our prayers, and he delights to answer. This does not mean God will always answer the way we would expect or want. It does mean he is able and we should come and ask with confident faith.

I have found that one area of big prayers that some Christians are reluctant to bring to God is healing prayers. What if I ask in faith and God does not heal? If the prayer is not answered the way I think it should be, is it because I lack faith? Some very sincere followers of Jesus resist asking for God's healing.

I encourage you to always ask of God. Cry out to him in faith and declare your trust. Express that you know God has the power to heal and restore. Dare to ask for God's healing touch. At the same time, place yourself and those you love in the hands of the Sovereign God who is wiser than you are. Declare your faith that God can heal and also your faithfulness to him if he decides not to heal. We don't raise a fist at God and demand healing. We come with humble hearts and ask for God to do what only he can accomplish. We also keep following him and praising him when he heals and when he does not.

FRIENDSHIP AND HEALING PRAYERS

Marce is a close friend who has gone through more surgeries than almost anyone I have ever met. She also has a relentlessly resilient and joyful spirit. She does not complain but places her faith in Jesus each day, walks with him, and prays for healing with faith-filled confidence. We have become friends and prayer partners over the years.

One day I was talking with Marce on the phone. She shared that she had just gotten the report on another CT scan and they had found a spot on her back. We prayed for her. I was getting ready for a second epidural that the doctor had recommended to try to relieve some of the constant pain in my leg and back. She prayed for me. We both asked God for healing—a big prayer. We also both confessed to God that we would love and follow him if we did not experience the healing we desired.

It is hard to put into words how sweet this experience was.

Both Marce and I love Jesus. We live and walk in faith, even when walking is painful. We rejoice with each other in times of healing or when one of us experiences relief from pain or receives a great report from a doctor. We comfort each other when the pain continues and the future seems uncertain. In all situations we keep praying big prayers with big faith.

MY GRACE IS SUFFICIENT

I lived with chronic pain for two years. I pressed on, but pain was a constant uninvited guest every day. I regularly prayed for healing, sometimes through tears. I prayed in faith and trust. I prayed for God's will in my life. Finally, my doctor told me he really believed I needed a surgery that would remove two of the ruptured discs in my neck and replace them with titanium discs that would be set into my vertebrae. I prayed that there would be some way we could afford this surgery, as many others had success with this procedure.

One problem was the surgery needed a couple more years of trials before insurance would cover part of the cost. We would have to pay for the entire surgery in cash and we did not have nearly enough money.

We kept praying. Over the coming months, a number of things happened. A few friends heard about the need and offered to help with the cost of the surgery. Another friend who works in the medical community helped find ways to reduce some of the costs. My doctor and physical therapist offered to reduce their fees as well. Kevin and I were able to come up with the remaining portion. I had the surgery and it was successful!

Over the next couple of years God opened the door to a series of amazing friendships through my surgery and recovery. We have become good friends with my surgeon and his wife. We have also become like family with the team at the physical therapist's office. I am so thankful for the excellent care I received through them. My life has been enriched through these relationships more than I could have imagined.

I think of the apostle Paul praying for God to remove his thorn in his flesh (2 Cor. 12:8). God's response was, "My grace is sufficient for you, for my power is made perfect in weakness" (2 Cor. 12:9). I have prayed big prayers for healing in my life and the lives of people I love. There have been times when God's answers were nothing short of miraculous. There have been other times God has said no to my prayer, but he has also unleashed his amazing grace in surprising ways and it is always enough.

THE REST OF THE STORY

While I was speaking at the women's conference in Adelaide, Australia, I decided to tell all the women about how God had answered Alma's "koala prayer." It was such a sweet story and I knew it would encourage them to pray about little things and big things in their lives. In the middle of my koala story, a murmur started in part of the room and began to spread like wildfire. Women were whispering, pointing, and giggling. As a communicator, I knew I had lost their attention. The women were no longer looking at me; they were all looking out a large window just behind me.

I turned around to see what had grabbed their attention. There on the branch of a eucalyptus tree was a very large, very cute, eyes-wide-open koala who had positioned himself right behind and above my head as I was telling my story. The koala was staring right into the room and looking at the women and me.

Before you knew it, women were out of their seats, they had cameras out, they were delighting and rejoicing in this wonderful moment. Some of them had rarely seen a koala and never one this big and wide awake in the middle of the day (it is very unusual for koalas to be seen in the daytime with eyes wide open). We all had a sense that this was another answer to a prayer about a small thing. God was giving us a sweet reminder that he answers prayers, both big and small.

YOUR PRAYER JOURNEY

Think about some small thing that just might bring a blessing to someone you know. Begin praying about it. Keep lifting it up and asking for God to surprise, bless, and show his love to this person. Try texting or emailing a prayer to someone in your life. I don't mean send them a text saying, "I will pray for you" (although that is good to do at times too). Instead, send your prayer. I have a dear friend, Nancy, who will often pray Scripture. When we can't get together to pray, Nancy will send text messages with a prayer or a Scripture prayer. Here is a recent text she sent me: "Hi Sherry, praying for you . . . 'Therefore I have hope. The Lord's loving kindnesses indeed never cease, for His compassions never fail. They are new every morning; great is Your faithfulness.' 'The Lord is my portion.' Says my soul, 'Therefore I have hope in Him' Lamentations 3:21-24."

Take time this week and text or email a prayer to someone in your life.

Chapter Sixteen

SOMETHING HAPPENS EVERY TIME YOU PRAY

*We can do nothing without prayer. All things can
be done by importunate prayer. It surmounts or
removes all obstacles, overcomes every resisting force
and gains its ends in the face of invincible hindrances.*
—E. M. Bounds

OUR FAMILY was on a short-term mission trip in the Netherlands with a team from our church partnering with a wonderful congregation, Crossroads International Church, in Amstelveen. The church had been setting up and tearing down in a rented facility for many years and had grown to be one of the largest congregations in the country. Our team came to lead worship, provide preaching, help out with the setup and teardown, and do some leadership training for two weekends.

On a few of the weekdays, we spent time inviting people to church and seeking to build relationships with people in the community and congregation. Our time reaching out to unchurched people seemed to bear very little fruit. The Netherlands is radically post-Christian, and when people heard we were from a church, many simply shut down and walked away.

At the end of each day, Kevin and I would gather our three sons and debrief. One evening we asked our boys, "What did you learn today?" Our middle son, Josh, who was twelve at the time, said, "Something happened every time we prayed." There was confidence in his tone and words.

I was surprised because I was not feeling as optimistic as he was. Honestly, I was a little concerned that this might end up being a discouraging mission trip experience for the boys. I had focused on the rejection and how most people were not very interested in church or conversations about faith. But Josh went on to recount how all through the day we had prayed and each time God did something. At times it was small and at times it was big, but Josh was right.

Josh reminded us that when we had car troubles at the start of the day, we prayed and we figured out how to solve the problem. He observed that when we went out to invite people to church, most were not interested, but there were a few people who seemed a little interested and, even though only one couple said they might come, that was at least two people who might visit the church on Sunday.

I had missed it, but Josh had not. Something happened every time we prayed. It might not have been what I wanted or expected, but God was clearly present and on the move.

There was spiritual activity, fruitfulness, or some kind of divine intervention each time we prayed. The words of my twelve-year-old son have stuck with me for more than two decades. His words encourage me to this day. We may not always see it, but God's power is released and something happens every single time we pray.

SURPRISING ANSWERS

If we live with confidence that something happens every time we pray, we will learn to recognize and be amazed by God's surprising answers to our daily prayers. But if we expect God to always answer the way we think he should, we will miss the glory and wonder of God's creative responses.

The Bible is full of surprising answers to prayer. When Peter was thrown into prison by the insane whim of King Herod, he would have been praying for release, comfort, and hope in what looked like a hopeless situation. Just a short time earlier, Herod had arrested James (the brother of John) and had him executed (Acts 12:1–2). One of Jesus' closest friends had been martyred. James was in the inner circle of disciples that Jesus invested in and mentored intimately. The other two were John and Peter. There is no way Peter would have felt safe or assured that he would leave prison alive.

Herod had arrested him and thrown him in jail because he saw that the religious leaders took delight when James was killed. Herod had Peter put under the guard of sixteen soldiers. One fisherman-turned-evangelist needed four squads of soldiers to guard him. Herod's plan was to do a quick trial after the Festival of Unleavened Bread and then have Peter killed also. It seemed his death was inevitable (Acts 12:3–4).

There was just one little wrinkle in Herod's plan. The church was earnestly praying for Peter (Acts 12:5). The prayers of God's people were ascending to heaven like incense. God heard. God acted.

Remember, something happens every time we pray. This time, the something that happened was extraordinary. It was more than any of the people could have imagined or dreamed . . . including

Peter. It is not that they lacked faith. But what God did was so far beyond their imagination that they would not have had a category for the kind of answer they received.

Peter was imprisoned in a locked cell with sixteen soldiers ready to stop any escape or jailbreak. Two of these soldiers were chained to Peter, one on each side of him. Sentries were at the door. There was no way out. Or so it seemed (Acts 12:6).

God's people were praying and things were about to get very interesting! The night before Peter was to go on trial and mere hours before Peter was to be accused and executed, heaven opened and God showed up to answer those prayers in a surprising way.

An angel appeared and radiated piercing light in the cell where Peter was incarcerated. The angelic being poked Peter, waking him up, then spoke to Peter and told him to get up. Peter's chains fell off his wrists. The angel then told Peter to get dressed and follow him out of the jail. They walked past the guards without being noticed. The iron gate swung open on its own accord. Peter followed the angel until he was out of the prison. Then the angel just . . . disappeared!

Something real happened when God's people prayed. Miracles unfolded. It was so staggering that Peter thought he was having a dream—even he did not think it was real. When the angel finally vanished and Peter realized he was free, he understood that he had been miraculously saved. Something happens when God's people pray, sometimes more than we are prepared for. When Peter came to the house where God's people were praying, they did not believe it was possible he was free and standing at the door. Even though they were praying, they were stunned and had to be convinced that Peter was there and alive (Acts 12:12–17).

When we read a story like this, we might get excited and assume that every time we pray, the answer will be a series of astounding miracles that lead to complete and immediate deliverance. That would be nice, but it is not what the Bible teaches. Something happens every time we pray, but things don't always play out exactly as we ask or expect.

Think about another great biblical leader who was also faithful and a man of prayer. The apostle Paul served Jesus with passion and total surrender. Over his years of ministry he faced great hardships, persecution, physical beatings, loneliness, rejection, and much more (2 Cor. 12:1–10). At one point, in utter honesty and transparency, Paul wrote about his struggle with what he called his "thorn in my flesh." After receiving "these surpassingly great revelations," he explained, "in order to keep me from becoming conceited, I was given a thorn in my flesh, a messenger of Satan, to torment me. Three times I pleaded with the Lord to take it away from me" (2 Cor. 12:7–8).

We don't know exactly what Paul's thorn in the flesh was, but it was so bad that he cried out to God, over and over, for deliverance and for it to be removed. We might expect God to do a miracle and answer his prayer by taking it away. After reading about Peter's shocking release from prison with an angelic guide, we might assume that God would remove the thorn immediately.

This is not what happened.

But we know that something happens every time we pray. God always hears. He loves his children. He is all-powerful. So what did God do as an answer to Paul's heartfelt prayer? Are you ready? Here it is. God said to him, "My grace is sufficient for you, for my power is made perfect in weakness" (2 Cor. 12:9). No angel. No shackles falling off or thorns being removed. No immediate deliverance and spontaneous songs of praise for an undeniable miracle.

Instead, God promised grace. God offered Paul power to make it through the torment of his thorn in the flesh. The thorn would stay, but so would God's grace. In that moment God said, "Let my presence and power be enough for you."

Paul's prayers were answered, but in a way very different from what he expected. He wanted the thorn gone. God said no. The Lord of creation knew that what Paul needed was power in weakness and grace in the pain of life.

Something happens every time you pray. For Peter, it was more than he expected. For Paul, the answer was different from what he wanted but exactly what he needed. As we walk through life, praying with our lives wide open, praying for people and with people, praying for small things and big things, we can be assured that something will happen every time we pray. We can also be certain that God's answers will rarely look exactly like what we imagine or expect.

GOD GETS THE GLORY

Jack Kuhatschek and Rod Jansen are both passionate followers of Jesus and fantastic leaders in the Christian publishing world. We have known Jack for more than two decades and consider him not only a partner in publishing but a close personal friend.

During a meeting to discuss the possible publishing of this book, Jack asked me, with bold frankness, "How is this book about prayer going to be different from all the other prayer books out there?" I shared about the vision of helping people learn to pray all through their day. I introduced the idea of making praying with eyes wide open a normal part of prayer. Jack decided to challenge me with a real situation in his own life and why my proposed book on prayer would be a good one for him to read. He said, "Well, I have been trying to sell my house for more than three months, and my wife and I have prayed. The truth is we are not getting many calls from people who even want to look at the house, and those who look at it are not interested."

I responded as I normally do and said to him, "Well, let's pray right now. We don't need to close our eyes." Then I just started praying. It was short and to the point. I humbly asked God to bring a buyer and to help Jack and Sandy sell their house so they could make a move to their new home in Florida, where they would begin their retirement years. I asked for patience if the timing was going to be longer than they had planned. I prayed that God would do this for his own glory.

Jack, Rod, and Kevin joined with me in prayer, and I could sense the presence of God in that moment. I told Jack I would continue to pray for the sale of their home. When I got in the car to drive away from our meeting, I prayed again.

Only a few hours later that same afternoon, Jack got a call from his real estate agent telling him that two different parties wanted to look at the house. Jack told my husband, in something of a joking manner, that if one of those buyers ended up purchasing the house, he would personally endorse the book.

I later received this email:

Sherry,

Thanks so much for your prayers! We put our home on the market in late April and then went through a series of price reductions over the next few months. During that time we had very few showings and only two low offers. We met with you and Kevin, and you offered to pray for us. That afternoon I told you that our realtor contacted us and asked if they could have two showings that day (after your prayer). One of the couples who looked at the house that day ended up buying it!

Jack

I was so happy for Jack and Sandy. I did not see this as surprising or shocking. Something happens every time we pray, and this was the way God decided to answer that specific prayer. I was confident that God was being glorified through this answered prayer.

Here is a portion of an email I received from Jack a short time later:

> Sherry and Kevin,
>
> We closed on our home today—praise God! We can trace the buyers back to the very day you offered to pray for us, which is so encouraging to us.

Those words—"Praise God!"—jumped out at me. That is what it is all about, the glory of God. When we pray, trusting in faith, God gets the glory when he answers our prayers.

One wonderful personal ending to this story is that I had the privilege of having Jack as the acquiring editor of this book, though he has now officially retired. That, too, was an answer to one of my prayers as it was Jack who, many years earlier, had been the first person to encourage me to write a book.

Some years later we reached out to Baker publishing company and some friends at Zondervan publishing company as well. Though this book was originally published by Baker, we really wanted it to be a part of the family of Organic Outreach resources we had developed, all published by Zondervan. Both are amazing publishers who seek to glorify Jesus and strengthen the church. As Kevin and I prayed, we were delighted when Baker let us buy back the rights on this book and Zondervan was excited to rerelease it as *Organic Prayer* and make it part of the Organic Outreach resources being used by churches and Christians all over the world. Once again, God has answered our prayers.

PRAYERS LIKE INCENSE

Some years ago Kevin and I were speaking for a group of leaders at a denominational gathering in Cleveland, Tennessee. We were going to be with this group for an extended amount of time over a few days, so we began our time together by having everyone introduce themselves and share one detail of their life. As one gentle and sweet woman opened up, she shared she had just learned she had cancer. My heart ached for her and I wanted to pray. It seemed only right to pause and pray then and there. I asked the whole group if we might pray for this dear woman, thinking I would lead in a short prayer.

What happened next was surprising, and glorious. As I began to pray, every person in the room also prayed, but not silently. They all lifted their voices with passion and volume. In a matter of seconds I could hardly hear my own voice. What I learned later was that people from their church tradition would normally all pray out loud at the same time. At that moment, I kept praying, but I also wondered, *How will they know when we are done?* After a few minutes of unified expressive prayer, the volume went down and I said, "Amen!"

In the days that followed we prayed together many more times. I quickly got used to all the voices lifted up at the same time. In private, Kevin made a comment to me about how hearing the prayers of many voices lifted at the same time must be a little like what God hears. The Lord of glory hears all of our prayers lifted in a perpetual concert of praise, confession, lament, and supplication.

I love the picture in the book of Revelation where John writes, "The four living creatures and the twenty-four elders fell down before the Lamb. Each one had a harp and they were holding golden bowls full of incense, which are the prayers of God's people"

(5:8). Our prayers float up toward heaven like incense. Tens of thousands, hundreds of thousands, perhaps millions of prayers at any given moment ascending to the very throne room of God like sweet incense. What a picture! What a spiritual reality!

When we pray through the flow of each day, our heart's cry joins the prayers of God's people around the world. They are lifted up and God hears, he cares, he answers.

Something happens every time you pray. And God is glorified.

KEEP PRAYING

Years ago I was overwhelmed with the simple two-word verse "Pray continually" (1 Thess. 5:17). Now I have learned that this passage is not saying we have to pray every moment of every day, but we are invited to. This is a decision that becomes a lifestyle.

One "something" that is happening every time you pray is that you are expressing faithfulness to God. In Romans 12:12 the apostle Paul writes, "Be joyful in hope, patient in affliction, faithful in prayer." That is my desire for my life and for yours, "be faithful in prayer." To do this, we will pray in many places and circumstances. This means at times we will need to pray with our eyes wide open. As we do, prayer will become a lifestyle, like breathing. The more we pray, the more we will encounter God, hear from him, be transformed, and give him all the glory and praise he deserves.

CLOSING PRAYER

God of all power who is present with his children at all times and in all places, teach us to pray in the normal flow of life. Open our eyes to see the pain of this world and pray for your healing touch. Let us see how you are moving in wonderful and glorious ways to share your love. Help us notice where you are at work and moving and pray for your glory to be revealed. Open our ears to hear your voice and follow your leading. Move our hands to action birthed in prayer. Transform our lives so that we are ever surrendered to your will and ways. Thank you that you hear our prayers, large and small, that you care, that you answer according to your perfect will. Father, Son, and Holy Spirit, we are your children. Teach us, lead us, and remind us each day that if we pray with our eyes wide open, our time with you is limitless. In the powerful name of Jesus. Amen!

YOUR PRAYER JOURNEY

Start a journal of simple prayers of thanks for answered prayers you have experienced. What has God done in response to your prayers or the prayers of people you love? As you identify how God has moved, answered, or shown up, give him thanks for being a God who hears and works on our behalf. You might want to share some of the answered prayers with Christian friends and even with people you love who are not yet followers of Jesus.

ACKNOWLEDGMENTS

KEVIN, THIS BOOK has come from my heart and life experience, but God has used your gifts as a writer to help shape my words and to make this book come alive. For your prayers, your partnership, your encouragement, and your relentless energy, I give praise to God.

Zach, Josh, and Nate, for more than three decades you have lived in a home that has been a laboratory of organic prayer. As my sons, you patiently let me pray for you countless times. Then you prayed with me through life's joys and trials. Now you each pray for me, and I am deeply grateful for the faith in Jesus and confidence in the power of prayer that we share together.

Christine, Taylor, and Brynne, you have become family, as one by one you have fallen in love with my sons. Thank you for your encouragement, your partnership in prayer, and the blessings you have become to our family.

Coen, Piper, Kell, Isla, and Ronan, you bless this grandma every time you let me teach you about prayer, and my heart soars every time I hear you pray.

The congregations of Corinth Reformed Church and Shoreline Church have been partners in the development of this book. Each of God's people in these churches who have prayed with me and for me has been a valuable and loved partner in this project.

Marilyn Hontz, Nancy Grisham, Lee Strobel, Joshua Ryan Butler, and Adam Barr are author friends who have spoken timely words and lifted up prayers that have spurred me onward in the writing of this book. Thanks to each of you.

Lucille Patmos, Patrice Glithero, and Nancy Kreer are my mentors and mighty women of God who have fought on my behalf, laboring in prayer and lifting me up through the writing of this book.

Ryan Pazdur has been a partner in the gospel for close to three decades. Through Zondervan and HarperCollins Christian Publishing he has given editorial leadership and pastoral insight into all five of the books in the Organic Outreach series. His keen insight and heart to see people come to faith in Jesus inspire me. A special thanks to the whole Zondervan Reflective team, especially Alexis De Weese and Brian Phipps.

The prayers of God's people ascend to the God of heaven like sweet incense. Thank you all for joining me in the privilege and delight of exalting the God who loves us and hears all we pray, anywhere, anytime, and in any circumstance. May we all experience more of God's presence and power through our prayers.

ABOUT THE AUTHOR

SHERRY HARNEY is an author and speaker who serves as the spiritual development director at Shoreline Church in Monterey, California. She is also the cofounder of Organic Outreach International, a ministry that trains church and movement leaders to mobilize their members to go into their communities and the world to share the good news of Jesus. For three decades, Sherry has spoken for local, national, and international groups and events. She focuses on prayer, spiritual formation, leadership, and organic outreach. She and her husband, Kevin, have coauthored books and partnered in writing small-group study guides with writers such as Ann Voskamp, Max Lucado, Gary Thomas, Rebekah Lyons, John Ortberg, Mark Batterson, Christine Caine, and Dallas Willard.

NOTES

1. Jonathan Edwards, "The Most High a Prayer-Hearing God," in *The Works of Jonathan Edwards, A. M.*, vol. 2 (London: Ball, Arnold, and Co., 1840), 116.

2. John Piper, *God's Passion for His Glory: Living the Vision of Jonathan Edwards* (Wheaton, IL: Crossway, 1998), 43.

3. Dallas Willard, session at the National Pastors' Conference.

4. Samuel Chadwick, in Nick Harrison, *Magnificent Prayer* (Grand Rapids: Zondervan, 2001), 365.

5. Brennan Manning also tells this story in his book *Abba's Child: The Cry of the Heart for Intimate Belonging* (Colorado Springs: NavPress, 1994), 46.

6. A. W. Tozer, *The Knowledge of the Holy* (New York: HarperOne, 1978), 1.

7. Dietrich Bonhoeffer, *Psalms: The Prayer Book of the Bible* (Minneapolis: Augsburg Fortress, 1970).

8. This structure is taken from Bernhard W. Anderson with Steven Bishop, *Out of the Depths: The Psalms Speak for Us Today* (Philadelphia: Westminster Press, 1983), 76–77.

9. Max Lucado, *You'll Get through This* (Nashville: Thomas Nelson, 2013), 29.

10. Klyne Snodgrass, *The NIV Application Commentary: Ephesians* (Grand Rapids: Zondervan, 1996), 344.

11. Max Lucado, *Before Amen: The Power of a Simple Prayer* (Nashville: Thomas Nelson, 2014), 75.

12. Charles Stanley, *Handle with Prayer* (Wheaton, IL: Victor, 1986), 95.

13. A. W. Tozer, *Tozer on the Almighty God: A 365-Day Devotional* (2004; Chicago: Moody, 2020), 21.

14. C. S. Lewis, *The Weight of Glory* (1949; San Francisco: HarperOne, 2001), 26.

15. Ron Dykstra, *Clean Jokes, Inspirational Stories, and More: A Collection by Ron Dykstra* (Oklahoma: Tate Publishing and Enterprises, 2009), 26–27.